HOUSE

SECRETS

APRIL CASTLE

MAPLE
PUBLISHERS

House of Secrets

Author: April Castle

Copyright © April Castle (2024)

The right of April Castle to be identified as author of this work has been asserted by the author in accordance with section 77 and 78 of the Copyright, Designs and Patents Act 1988.

First Published in 2024

ISBN: 978-1-83538-095-6 (Paperback)

978-1-83538-096-3 (E-Book)

Book layout and cover by:

White Magic Studios
www.whitemagicstudios.co.uk

Published by:

Maple Publishers
Fairbourne Drive, Atterbury,
Milton Keynes, MK10 9RG, UK
www.maplepublishers.com

Dedication

This book is dedicated to my Dad and Drew

Author
April Castle

Contents

There are no secrets better kept than the secrets that everybody guesses.

George Bernard Shaw

Introduction

In the pages that follow a remarkable story unfolds. It's a story that delves into the depths of a complex relationship and which ultimately shapes the life of a courageous individual.

April Castle's captivating debut memoir witnesses the unravelling of an intricate web spun by a lying and manipulative mother.

This memoir is much more than just the tale of a deceptive mother. It is a tapestry that is woven with the threads of life's unexpected events. House fires, theft, illness and the weight of death all leave indelible marks on Aprils journey. Her resolve and resilience are constantly tested.

As you turn the pages you will embark on a journey that spans from April's innocent childhood through to her tumultuous teenage years and adulthood. You will follow her journey as she navigates her way through a landscape of betrayal where truth and deception intertwine with the most devastating consequences.

This is an emotional rollercoaster where heartache and triumph coexist.

April Castle openly bares her soul with unflinching honesty, inviting you, the reader, to bear witness to the intricacies of her experiences.

Through April's own words you will discover the importance of forgiveness, the strength of perseverance, the power of resilience and the transformative ability to discover strength amidst the chaos.

Immerse yourself in the remarkable journey that is April Castle's memoir and discover the irony of the twists and turns in her life.

We hope you will find solace, inspiration and an unwavering reminder that even in the darkest of circumstances there is always, always, a glimmer of hope.

One Wedding and a Baby

Back in the 1960s there was a chance meeting between two young people. Their names were Sylvie and Frank. Sylvie was small in height with dark coloured hair and quite attractive in appearance. She worked every weekday at the Co-operative store in the centre of Newcastle as a retail assistant. She usually travelled to work on the number seven bus at the same time each day.

Frank, who was of a medium height with thick glossy dark hair, worked for the local bus company as a Ticket Collector. Although he worked on several different bus routes he was generally on the Number seven route - the very same route which Sylvie regularly travelled on.

When Frank saw Sylvie for the first time his eyes widened in awe and he took an instant shine to her. He couldn't help but be captivated by her beauty and radiant smile. As each day passed he would spend a little longer on issuing or checking her bus ticket because it provided an opportunity to have a brief chat with her. Sylvie was like a breath of fresh air to Frank and brought light to the mundane routine of his daily work.

As the days went by their brief chats turned into longer conversations and it was becoming clear that there was a real spark and connection between them. So, after a few weeks, Frank eventually plucked up the courage to ask Sylvie if she would like to go out on a date to the Majestic Dance Hall.

Sylvie seemed very flattered to have been asked out on a date and quickly agreed. On that very first date there was an instant attraction between them. They soon realised that they enjoyed each other's company and that their friendship was turning into love.

It wasn't long before they became an 'official' couple as friends and family gained knowledge about their courtship. As the weeks passed Frank and Sylvie were getting on like a house on fire and enjoying their special time together.

It was only a couple of months after meeting Frank that Sylvie started to feel unwell. Especially in the mornings. She started to suspect that maybe, just maybe, she could be pregnant.

Sylvie kept her suspicions to herself and didn't say a word to anyone. She hastily arranged a doctor's appointment. In her mind she was hoping that she had a bug or a virus but in her heart of hearts she knew that it could be something quite different.

Sylvie's emotions were mixed between excitement and trepidation as she walked the short journey to the surgery. She was scared, confused and worried. After arriving at the surgery, she calmly sat down in the waiting room. After only a few minutes, although it seemed like hours, her name was called out and she stood up and made her way to Doctor Kelly's room.

Dr Kelly asked her how he could help and she nervously told him that she thought she might be pregnant. Dr Kelly asked Sylvie to lie on the couch where he examined her and undertook a pregnancy test. He asked Sylvie to come and sit back in the chair. Sylvie sat quietly awaiting the news from the Doctor "Sylvie" he said "After completing my examination I can confirm that you are indeed pregnant'.

Sylvie quietly gasped, her heart was pounding in her chest and she felt quite light-headed. She thanked the Doctor for his time and diagnosis, got up from the chair and left the room as quickly as her feet could carry her.

Sylvie's suspicions were right! She was pregnant! 12 weeks pregnant - with me!

Sylvie felt an utter sense of panic and knew that she needed to tell Frank. She couldn't tell him by phone, this was something important and she needed to tell him in person.

Sylvie phoned Frank at his home saying that they needed to meet as she had something important, something special, that she needed to tell him. Frank tried his best to quiz her to try to find out what was so important but Sylvie wasn't giving anything away and said she needed to talk to him in person.

They agreed to meet up the next day after work. Frank was feeling apprehensive, worried and somewhat anxious. His initial thoughts were that Sylvie was going to break up with him and end their relationship.

Maybe she had fallen in love with another boy who had a better job than him and better prospects. All sorts of scenarios were whirling around in his head.

The following day, after work, they met up at the local pub. Sylvie stretched out her arm and took hold of Franks hand. Stroking his hand, she told him there was something really important that he needed to know. Frank was nervous and worried yet remained calm. Sylvie chose her words carefully and gently broke the news to Frank that she was 12 weeks pregnant.

Of all the scenarios that had gone through Franks head this was not one of them. This was really not what Frank was expecting to hear. The news about bringing a baby into the world would be life-changing.

Frank and Sylvie barely knew each other. Frank looked straight into Sylvie's eyes and could see that she was happy and smiling, not a forced smile but a truly beaming smile. To Frank she seemed almost overcome with joy that she was pregnant and had now shared the news with Frank, the love of her life and hoped that he felt the same about the news as she did.

Frank, however, didn't feel the same excitement as Sylvie and took a few moments to process what he had been told and to let the news sink in. Despite the shock, Frank composed himself. He was a man who took responsibilities seriously and he was honourable, just like his Father. He took Sylvie's hand and lovingly asked her to marry him. Sylvie could hardly contain her excitement and accepted his proposal of marriage without a moment's hesitation.

Once Sylvie and Frank got over their initial fears their emotions quickly turned to excitement. They started to plan their next steps – where they would live, how they would furnish their home but first, they needed to tell their parents. Frank, always the sensible one, suggested planning a small family gathering with both sets of parents being invited so that they could give them the news together.

Sylvie's eyes sparkled with excitement and she nodded in agreement. "that sounds perfect Frank! Let's make it a night that everyone will remember". They arranged to meet up at Franks family home on the Thursday night. Both sets of parents would be there.

Thursday night arrived and Frank and Sylvie were both very nervous but equally found it hard to contain their excitement. With both sets of parents waiting in anticipation and with Frank and Sylvie's, hearts pounding and hands trembling they took a deep breath, composed themselves and quietly told both sets of parents, in harmony, that they were going to have a baby and would be getting married.

In the quiet room you could hear intakes of breath and gasps and it seemed that time stood still, at least momentarily. After the initial shock, both sets of parents knew in their hearts that they needed to support their children so they soon started to warm to the idea of becoming grandparents. The families each decided to pull together to help with the impending wedding arrangements.

To Frank and Sylvie's relief both families embraced Frank and Sylvie and gave them their blessing along with lots of advice and do's and don'ts. The wedding was hastily arranged and invites sent out to close family and friends.

Sylvie pondered about what to wear but eventually decided on a pink fitted two-piece suit which would cover her growing baby bump. Her long dark hair was styled into a bouffant beehive which was very popular in the 1960's.

Frank bought a smart black pin striped suit with slim drainpipe trousers. He had his thick dark hair swept back into a Teddy Boy style with a flamboyant quiff to the front.

The wedding was a small affair. Frank was brought up a Catholic and was keen to marry in a Catholic Church which Sylvie was in agreement with. The church was in the West End of Newcastle and not far from where Sylvie's Mam lived.

The weather on the Wedding day was beautiful. The sun was shining and Frank and Sylvie looked relaxed and a very handsome couple as they arrived at the church. They were both young, Sylvie was only 19 years old and Frank was 21 but they seemed very much in love.

The wedding ceremony was short with only close family and friends looking on as Frank and Sylvie made their solemn commitment to each other. As the priest pronounced them Husband and Wife, Mr and Mrs Castle, Frank kissed his bride and they walked along the aisle arm in arm.

As they assembled with guests outside of the church there was no official photographer waiting but family and friends were ready and took photos as other guests showered the Bride and Groom with multi-coloured confetti. The couple enjoyed every moment of being in the spotlight on their very special day. As stormy clouds were swirling above, the wedding party headed over to Sylvie's Mam's for a buffet reception.

Sylvie's Mam put on a magnificent spread with a variety of sandwiches, pies, sausage rolls, quiche and cakes. There was plenty to drink too, including tea, coffee, soft drinks and beer. The room was full of chatter, laughter and joy and everyone was having a good time. Family and friends all raised their glasses to Frank and Sylvie wishing them a long and happy future together.

With the wedding over it was all hands-on deck by both sets of parents as they excitedly helped, guided and supported Frank and Sylvie in readiness for the impending arrival of a new baby.

And, sure enough, in 1966, just a matter of weeks after their wedding I was born. A baby girl that they named April.

In quite quick succession Mam and Dad went on to have two more children, my brothers, Robert and Alfie.

Chapter 2

A Blazing Start

I have very fond memories of my humble beginnings and my early years. Even today, they still hold a truly special place in my heart. My memories are not of extravagance or material possessions, just memories of times that were full of laughter, forging new friendships, playing games and having lots of simple adventures with friends, neighbours and family.

One simple pleasure that stands out amidst the complex tapestry of my childhood was Mam and Dads first home where I shared their bed and would sit and listen to the crackling sounds of the real coal fire that would often burn peacefully and bring warmth to the cold air.

I often found solace in the comforting glow of the fire burning in the fireplace at the bottom of the bed. At night, when the room was dark, I would be fascinated and mesmerized by the blazing flames with their ever-changing hues. They would change from a pale yellow to golden and then to a bright orange or a rich red. I would be captivated by the crackling sounds as they seemed to whisper their secrets. There was often a gentle breeze that sneaked through the edges of the bedroom door which would cause the flames to move and sway as though they were dancing to some invisible melody.

I don't know how long Mam and Dad had planned to live in their first home but it was dramatically and frighteningly cut short.

Somehow fate took its course and on one particular night a cinder escaped from the fire in the bedroom and landed on the worn wooden floorboards causing the wood to ignite. The fire burnt slowly and innocently at first but within moments the fire suddenly took hold with such a ferocity that it quickly began to rage throughout our home.

As the flames grew higher and higher and transformed our once welcoming home into a scene of chaos we could only watch in horror from the pavement outside. We could hear the sound of fire engines, their sirens blaring in the cold night air and moments later we watched as the blue flashing lights lit up the street as they raced towards our house.

Someone, I don't know who, had made an emergency phone call to 999 and requested the Fire Service. Thank goodness they did because their actions prevented the fire from spreading to neighbouring houses.

When the heroic firefighters arrived, they were met with a daunting sight. Our once serene and beautiful home was now enveloped in an angry blaze. The windows were glowing with an eerie intensity and as the flames continued to take hold the curtains gradually started falling from the windows.

The air was dark and thick with the acrid smell of smoke.

The firefighters were determined and focused with the task ahead of them. They quickly sprang into action, their training and experience falling into place and guiding their every move.

With precision and co-ordination, the firefighters unravelled their hoses, connecting them to the fire hydrant on the side of the road. The thunderous sound of the rushing water filled the atmosphere as the powerful jets of water were directed towards the inferno. The flames hissed and spat and slowly started to subside. Encased in their protective clothing they battled through the searing heat and into the house. They're single primary objective was to rescue any occupants who may still be in the house. Fortunately, everyone had escaped the house and were stood outside in the street. Sylvie and Frank were dazed but safe. They were horrified by what was happening before their very eyes.

When the firefighters gained access into the house what they found was a scene of complete devastation. The once familiar rooms were now unrecognisable and obscured by flames, dense smoke and charred debris. The men had skilfully and carefully manoeuvred their way through the house and had targeted the most ferocious areas of the fire. Their water hoses unleashed a torrential downpour, dousing the flames and creating a veil of steam that danced, just as the flames had, in the night air.

The firefighters did their best but our home was destroyed and could not be saved from the fiery fate. However, the tireless efforts of the men had managed to isolate the fire and prevent it from spreading to neighbouring homes.

We were shocked and stricken. We were homeless! The very next day Dad went to the local Council Offices asking for help to find a new home. He was told that there were no vacant houses nearby. We were devastated.

With houses and flats being in short supply or not being available at all we found ourselves seeking temporary refuge with Dad's parents who lived on the North side of Newcastle. My paternal grandparents, Alf and Annie embraced us with open arms. They comforted us and offered us a place to stay which provided us with a sense of stability during a time of immense upheaval and uncertainty.

Grandma and Grandad lived in a newly built house which was located just on the outskirts of Newcastle. It was certainly a bit of a tight squeeze with two families living in a small house but, somehow, we managed. We were so grateful to Grandma and Grandad. Mam was only young but I remember her telling me that it was during this time that Grandma taught her how to cook, how to clean and run a home as it should be.

As the hours turned into days, the days into weeks and the weeks into months Mam and Dad waited patiently for news of any vacant house or flat that could become theirs and a place that they could call home.

I remember admiring Mam and Dad around this time because, in the face of immense adversity, they still managed to show resilience, retain an unwavering determination to resolve the situation we were in whilst offering constant reassurances that everything would be ok.

After several long months of living with Grandma and Grandad a flat did become available in nearby Chester Close. We were all so excited. We were on the threshold of a new beginning, a fresh start. We could be a family again!

Mam and Dad were given the keys to the flat and they quickly started decorating it, one room at a time. They bought furniture and fittings and transformed the flat into a truly lovely family home.

Chester Close was made up of several 3 story blocks of flats which were set out in the formation of squares. The blocks were all mainly constructed in a cold looking grey concrete, not very attractive but quite practical. I find it quite strange that now concrete seems to be visually attractive and used in many loft type properties.

The streets surrounding the blocks were made up of several terraced properties and a few small semi-detached houses all of which had good-sized gardens to both the front and back. Local residents took pride in their gardens and in summer they would be full of colourful flowers.

Although the estate felt quite enclosed, being surrounded by houses and flats that were all built very close together, the estate was fully self-contained, so there was never a need to leave the estate to do shopping.

We were very fortunate to have a range of different shops and amenities and all within walking distance. Just along the road from our flat was the Red Lion pub where Grandma was Captain of the darts team. Across the street stood the Labour Club which was well known for its men's darts teams. The 1970's was a generation when working men's clubs were very much a place where men were allowed in the bar but women weren't. Women were only usually allowed in the Concert room.

The shopping centre stood proudly right in the middle of the estate and, much like the housing estate, it was built in a square shape. In the Centre you would find a good selection of small independent shops such as the newsagents where the local men would get their cigarettes and on a Saturday night they would get the Saturday Pink newspaper which contained all they needed to know about that day's football matches.

In the 1970's when the country suffered much industrial unrest there were many blackouts which meant no heat or light. I remember we would go to the hardware store to buy candles to provide light and tins of paraffin for the heaters. Next door to the hardware store was the Chippy and a wet fish shop.

The clothes store styling was very primitive with its makeshift changing room created by using a heavy curtain held up by a string. If you tried on any clothes you just hoped and prayed that the curtain didn't collapse! Nearby, was a wool shop where Grandma would often buy her wool to crochet, a supermarket, a butchers' where Mam always bought the pork chops, stewing beef and, for a special treat for Dad, some steak.

One of my favourite shops was Crawford's. We all loved Crawford's The Bakers because it's shelves were full of lots of lovely sweet treats such as fairy cakes and peach melbas as well as breads and stotties. There was also a fruiterer and a large freezer shop.

Nestled close to the shops was a range of NHS health services such as GP's, Clinics and Dentist as well as a community library and a Church. The shopping centre was really the beating heart of the estate. It was always busy as locals could get most of what they needed which prevented them from having to travel outside of the estate and incurring more cost.

A trip to the shops was always a really social affair and would take absolutely ages. The local women would stand and gossip whilst letting their children play safely in the large open spaces.

A popular place for children to play was the huge stone water fountain. Everyone told us it was a fountain although no water was ever seen to come out of it! Even so, it was great fun to clamber up onto the edge of the fountain's rim and attempt to walk around it without falling off. Getting your balance was a challenge. The trick was to fully stretch your arms out to the side, gently move forward by putting one foot directly in front of the other just as though you were a tightrope walker.

Our flat was on the middle floor of a three-story block. Getting to the flat could be a bit of a challenge, especially if you had bags of heavy shopping. To navigate your way to the flat you needed to negotiate14 twisting and turning stone steps with small landings that connected each of the floors to each other.

There was a communal front and back entrance into the block itself which led to the two ground floor flats and their front doors. There were fourteen stone steps leading to a landing which had the two middle floor flats and then another fourteen stairs leading to the two top floor flats and landing. Both sets of stairs had metal bannisters with railings which were great to slide down if you wanted a quick exit instead of negotiating all of the stairs.

We called the communal areas the 'passage' and this was also our play area on rainy days. We used to play 'houses' or 'Mam's and dads', on the different landings and we stored our bikes and prams under the stairwell. Some neighbours really took pride in their passage and they would scrub, swill and disinfect the concrete stairs each week and pin back the doorways so the wind could blow through and dry the stairs.

I remember seeing neighbours hanging their net curtains at the landing window and laying carpet runners along the landing with matching doormats at their front door. It was always a talking point and a bit of an unspoken competition to see who had the cleanest and tidiest passage. There was always gossip if someone had a dirty passage.

In the wintertime the open stairwells were always dark and cold and the wind would blow through the passage from the communal front and back doors. Sometimes it could feel really scary.

Flats on our Estate

Chapter 3

Family Life

For much of Frank and Sylvie's marriage we lived near to Dad's parents. They were very much involved in many aspects of our day-to-day family life. Dad was a real family man and would spend whatever time he could playing games with me and my brothers or using his amazing DIY skills to design, create and build or re-build things.

Dad was always hardworking. He got his work ethic from Grandad Alf. He always made it his priority to work hard so that he could provide for his family. Over the years Dad did various jobs but they were mainly practical jobs and manual work often on building sites. Initially he drove tipper trucks and then he started to work as a roofer.

Dad earned good money but when he was working locally he would often work very long hours to make good money. Sometimes his work took him to other parts of the country. He travelled all around the UK, and would be away during the week and return home at the weekend. On occasions Dad would work abroad, mainly in Arabic countries. You always knew when he was going to be working away as out came his passport and a huge mustard-coloured suitcase ready to be packed for the journey.

Dad knew the value of money and was good at saving. He made sure that whenever he bought something for himself, us or our home it was always of good quality and something that would last whereas Mam would just spend whatever money she had until it was gone and then she would want more. She could never settle knowing that Dad had savings.

Dad was quite a bit taller than Mam with a good strong head of brown hair, everyone thought he looked a bit like the famous singer Frank Sinatra because he had the same blue eyes. Dad was great, he was thoughtful, motivated, friendly, caring and very patient.

He was very practical and had lots of different skills which meant he could turn his hands to many DIY jobs such as painting, decorating, mending and making. In his spare time, he particularly enjoyed making small plaster of Paris objects such as animals. I often helped Dad to paint them before they were displayed on a wooden cubed box that he'd made some years ago and which was hung on the wall in the sitting room. Mam didn't appreciate the work that went into the beautiful animal figurines and was quite disinterested.

Even in the 1970's Dad was a recycling warrior making lots of useful items from discarded or unused materials.

Dad made Go-Carts for me, Robert and Alfie and they were really ingenious. He made them from recycled wood and any other bits and pieces he could find. The Go-cart had a front axle that allowed us to steer to the right and left, the wheels were from old prams because their rubber tyres were really thick and sturdy and could cope with the rough terrain on the estate.

Dad attached a really strong rope to the front of the cart which you gripped tightly with both hands and used this to steer the cart, next he attached pedals on the base to help get the cart moving and also, importantly, to stop it. The wooden seats would be quite hard and uncomfortable so Dad upholstered them using scraps of old carpets and cushions. The carts were amazing and we had *so* much fun.

Mam, on the other hand, had a very different personality and approach to Dad. She was much more self-centred, selfish and quite independent. She would always put her needs first before thinking of Dad or us. Her needs were always the number one priority.

There were times when she would make you feel as though she didn't want you around, that you were in the way, or you were a nuisance. If you ever dared to ask any personal question her face would redden, her teeth would clench and she would glower and grimace and then send you off to your bedroom or to play outside.

Mam was never very social with Dad's family other than our Saturday get-togethers where we went to Grandma and Grandads' house and met up with Uncle Laurie, Dad's brother-in-law, Auntie Jeannie, Dad's sister and our cousins for Cabbage, Tatties and Ham. Other than that Mam never wanted to join in with any family activities or trips out. She would always say she had something else she needed to do but we never knew what that was.

Mam was always very temperamental and her mood would change from day to day or, sometimes, from hour to hour, particularly if she couldn't get what she wanted. She was always very needy and this would often be the cause of arguments, loud and angry arguments, hostile arguments with Mam breaking crockery and throwing cushions in her fury and frustration. Dad would be steadfast and only ever retaliate with words which were spoken at a raised but monotone level in an attempt to calm Mam down.

Often the calming words didn't work, and Mam would become even angrier and even more frustrated and would hurl any object that she could grasp from around the room.

The arguments usually centred around money. Mam was very much motivated by money, she loved money and was always keen to have more money so that she could buy or replace things that we already had. If she couldn't get her own way she would use tactics of lies, manipulation and deceit.

If Mam wanted something new you would notice that items within the house would suddenly start to malfunction. As an example: electrical items would suddenly stop working rips and tears would appear in cushions and bedding and the springs in the sofa would start to emerge through the cushions.

Mam was always determined and very convincing in her pursuit for dominance so, more often than not, she was able to convince me and my brothers that it was Dad who was mean, unreasonable and in the wrong. We knew Dad worked hard to earn money to support the family and we knew that he was careful with money. Dad was always a saver rather than a spender but that didn't make him mean. He would often spend money on me and my brothers but when he did he spent it wisely and he spent it well.

I remember Mam asking Dad for money to buy our new school uniforms. Dad was more than happy to give her the money she needed for the uniforms and gave her a wad of cash. But Mam could be very devious and instead of using the money to buy the uniforms she kept the cash for herself and took out a Provident loan. Provident were a large financial company that offered loans which could be repaid on a weekly basis. A local representative would call at houses to collect the repayments.

I remember Mr. Milburn, one of the representatives from Provident, would come around to our house each Friday, regular as clockwork, to collect the payments. Mam was always stood at the door waiting for his arrival. She would quickly hand over the payment and Mr Milburn would fill in payment details on a card and that was the weekly transaction complete.

Dad knew nothing about the Provident loans. Dad always paid his way and would never borrow money but when Dad found out that Mam had spent the money he had given her and taken out a loan he was furious and it resulted in the most vociferous argument that I had ever heard.

Some years later Mam took on a part-time job working for Provident. She was the one who would now collect weekly payments from people on the estate on behalf of Provident except …. she collected the money but didn't actually hand it over to Provident. She kept it for herself. Eventually she was found out and Dad, being the honest and honourable man that he was, got her out of the trouble she was in by paying back all of the money that was owed to Provident.

This caused yet more arguments with Mam accusing Dad of not giving her enough money. Mam was always the victim. Sometimes the arguments were so bad that me, Robert and Alfie became scared and would escape the noise and volatility by playing outside or, if the noise wasn't too loud, we would escape into our bedrooms.

I'm imagining that you now have an image in your head of my Mam as being a large, confident and bold woman with a brusque and aggressive nature. Well, that would be quite wrong. She's exactly the opposite. Mam is small in stature, you could even say she is petite. She has a charismatic personality, can be very charming, kind and generous - to everyone but us! But, behind the façade, what others didn't realise, was the charm Sylvie exuded was wholly superficial. The *real* Sylvie was deceitful, dishonest, hurtful and manipulative and without a moral compass.

There is no doubt that Mam is an attractive woman and I can completely see why Dad fell in love with her. She was a creature of habit and, for most of her life, she has worn her thin highlighted blond hair in a short style. Her hair had a natural soft and gentle curl to the back which could cause it to flick up at the ends. I can remember her standing at the mirror each morning with her long brown comb backcombing her hair until it looked thicker, fuller and had more height.

Mam 's skin was pale in colour but she didn't wear make-up - no foundation, no blusher no eyeshadow no eyeliner. In fact, I don't think she knew how to apply makeup as she never made any effort to enhance her facial features but she was naturally very pretty. I wouldn't say Mam was glamorous but she always looked clean, smart and neatly dressed.

Mam wasn't a drinker or a smoker either but she loved to listen to music and particularly liked Tom Jones. Whenever a Tom Jones record would come on the radio her eyes would light up and she would sing along to the song and have a little dance.

Mam went to see Tom Jones in concert several times. In more recent years when my brother was working in a club in Newcastle that was providing hospitality for Tom Jones he asked if Tom would speak to Sylvie on his mobile phone. Tom phoned Sylvie and asked if she had enjoyed the show. Sylvie was speechless but thoroughly enjoyed her moment of fame. My brother had his photo taken with Tom Jones and this took pride of place in the living room alongside the glass Tom had drunk from in the club.

Mam didn't really have any hobbies but from time to time she would enjoy knitting. If I'm honest I think her real hobby was getting and spending money. Sometimes the money she was spending wasn't her money and this got her into trouble on more than one occasion.

From time-to-time Mam would work part time cleaning offices but she never seemed to hold down a job for any great length of time and seemed to dip in and out of different jobs. I remember her working in different shops like the off-licence and the Red Lion pub where she met new acquaintances, some with a dubious background.

It was when Mam was working part-time in the local Off-Licence that there was a robbery. As part of Mam's responsibilities, she had to cash up the till at the end of her shift and put that day's takings into a bag to take to the bank.

On one particular evening Mam finished her shift, cashed up the takings, locked up the shop taking the money with her and started walking towards home when a person came up and grabbed her from behind pulling her down to the ground. Whoever it was then ran off towards Newcastle with that day's takings in their hands. Fortunately, Mam wasn't hurt just a bit shaken and brushed the incident off as though it had never happened. We were all shocked!

Mam said she did not get a look at the robber as they had approached her from behind but the owner of the shop contacted the Police and reported the incident.

No-one was questioned or arrested for the robbery but many years later it came to light that Mam and her brother had forged a plan together to fake the robbery at the off-licence and keep the takings for themselves.

Chapter 4

Fun and Fear

Where we lived was a bit like a concrete jungle. It was a fascinating but dull blend of urban design with a strong and sturdy grey construction. Even though all the neighbours were nice and friendly and I generally felt quite safe I can remember being particularly scared on one occasion.

I was returning home after picking up some bread that Mam had asked me to get from the shops. It was winter-time and just at that point when the night sky was dark from early evening right through until 7am in the morning.

I can clearly remember that night, as though it was yesterday. I remember the dark, dank sky, the whistle of the wind along the shadowy stairwell, the dismal grey concrete looking damp and dark from days of rain and the echoing sounds of mysterious feet scraping and shuffling against the stone stairs as they slowly moved around. It felt like the footsteps were following me, the faster I moved the faster the footsteps seemed to move.

In a panic I started to run up the stairs two by two. I was feeling anxious and breathing heavily, my hands were gripping the metal handrails as I swung around each of the landing corners until I finally reached my own front door. Almost out of breath and feeling faint I quickly pushed down on the door handle, pushed it open and ran inside quickly slamming the door behind me and breathing a huge sigh of relief that I was at home, safe and behind closed doors.

The experience of this day made me be extra vigilant when I was going out and about. The communal entrances were open for anyone to access and there was a time when we were told about a man who had been seen exposing himself somewhere around the ground floor communal entrance.

This man was known as 'The Flasher' and would appear, from time to time, at different blocks of flats. It really scared me and my friends so we all played close to our homes and stayed together in groups to be safe

Mam would often ask me to run errands and go to the shops and, on one particular day, just as I left our flat and started to go down the stairs, I was suddenly struck by the thought that the flasher could be under the stairs. I leant over the banister to see if he was there and he was! I could see his shoes and his feet move. I just froze! I stumbled but quickly turned around and fled back upstairs. I was petrified, terrified. I rushed into our flat and told Mam that the flasher was under the stairs.

Without a moment's hesitation Mam swung into action and picked up one of our heavy wooden rounders bats and raced down the stairs raising the bat high as she rounded the stairs. Breathing heavily, I watched as Mam descended the stairs, getting ever closer to where the flasher was. Suddenly, I heard a man screech, then, for a brief moment there was complete silence, followed by laughter. Loud laughter that echoed rhythmically through the corridors. The person Mam had approached whilst wielding a rounders bat wasn't the flasher. It was Rocky, the window cleaner!

Rocky the window cleaner was a very talented rockabilly singer and was loved by everyone on the estate. He was tall, and slim with Elvis Presley style hair complete with sideburns and nicely tanned skin.

Rocky enjoyed a cigarette and, in between cleaning windows, he would take the opportunity for a quick cigarette under the stairs in our block of flats. Mam and Rocky saw the funny side of things and Rocky apologised for making me scared but it took quite a while before my heartbeat returned to normal and I could see the funny side of things.

The flats all had their scary nooks and crannies but they were also very practical. On the ground floor each flat had a tall, slim, built-in general storage cupboard where you could keep outdoor toys or bikes. We would use it to store the go-carts that Dad made and also our bikes. Mam and Dad would also use it to store odds and ends, mainly anything which wasn't likely to get damaged or go missing - things often went missing!

Although the flats in Chester Close, were very similar in design, they were distinguished by their front doors which were all coloured differently.

Outside of the flats on the ground floor were two large brick built drying areas. Each of the flats had their own dedicated drying area where laundry could be hung to dry. This was a great place to play 'chasey' as we would run through all of the washing which was drying on the line.

Separating the brick drying areas were two large grassed areas where me and my two brothers, Robert and Alfie, could play. There were lots of children of all ages living in the different square blocks, and we all played and went to the same local school together. Lots of different games were played depending on the season. It could be football or conkers or Liggies (marbles) or Tag. I remember we spent hours and hours playing competitive games of Liggies.

The drying areas and grass areas were also built in a square shape and, if you were to have an aerial view, everything was in a block and we referred to our little world outside as the block. We rode our bike around the block, we raced our go carts around the block. We played hide and seek within our block. We played knocky nine doors, a game where you would knock on someone's door and then run away quickly before they saw you. Adults found it annoying but we loved it although we generally got caught and into trouble.

We would always have a huge bonfire on 'Bonnie night'. We would search for the perfect and safe spot on the grassed area within our block where we could build the bonfire and start collecting the bonnie wood. We stored the wood in the storage cupboards in the passage, making sure it was safe from bonnie raiders who would be out to steal bonnie wood for their own fire.

Every block had their own bonfire, and we were all very territorial when we were collecting bonnie wood and storing it. Neighbours would get rid of old wooden furniture like beds and wardrobes around bonfire night and we would collect them and pile it all high ready for the stack. Some of the bonfire stacks were huge and thinking about it now I'm sure health and safety probably wouldn't allow it.

The building of the bonfire itself was a real skill and quite an art form. We would start by creating a sturdy base with larger bits of bonnie wood forming a sort of a circular shape and then carefully stack smaller bits of wood on top to create a sort of tepee-like structure. When we had built it as high as we could we would put some newspaper and kindle wood in the bottom to help the wood ignite.

We always had a Guy for the top of the stack. We would make a Guy using newspaper for stuffing the arms, legs and body, old clothes to cover the make-shift body, tying string around it to keep everything in place. We made a mask for the face and put an old hat, tied with a rope, on the head.

We would put the Guy into an old pram and push him around the estate asking 'penny for the Guy. We would start with knocking on doors around our block or sometimes we would wait outside of the pub or club asking customers as they went in, if they had a penny for the Guy. We would often make enough money to share it out between us to buy sweets, pop or chips from the chippy. Once we'd collected as much as we could the Guy was firmly placed on the top of our huge bonfire until he met his fate.

It could be great fun living on our estate, especially at Bonnie time and when I was really young and didn't have any responsibilities. I enjoyed playing outside and I enjoyed playing in our flat with my Sindy dolls even though I shared a bedroom with my brothers. Our flat was really nice, except for the yellow front door!

From the outside the flat looked small but once inside it was quite spacious, apart from the kitchen. Our front door was a sort of pale yellow in colour which I wasn't very keen on because it always seemed to attract flies, wasps and bees.

Just outside of the front door we had a small balcony which looked on to the drying blocks and grassed area. The bees always seemed to head straight across the balcony and towards our yellow front door. In the summer months I would be waving my arms about as I tried to get into the house without taking additional buzzing guests.

When we were altogether, we would spend family time in the sitting room as it was the only room that was quite large and where we could all be together. Dad had spent a lot of time over the years making the house look nice and just how Mam wanted it to be. He would spend most weekends doing some form of DIY, either painting, decorating or making household items.

Mam had always wanted wood panelling in the sitting room, so Dad bought packs of panelling and carefully and meticulously fitted the wooden panelling to the walls. It looked lovely against the tiled fireplace with its open fire, mantle and hearth. There was always a highly polished brass Companion set comprising of a brush, shovel and poker sat neatly on the hearth. The brush had definitely seen its better days and was very worn with lots of missing bristles, but it was still functional. The brass poker was all black and charred at the end from many years of use.

We had a coal cupboard on the veranda and the coal man would deliver bags of coal each week. He would carry a huge, heavy sack of coal on his back up the 14 stairs and then tip it straight into the coal cupboard leaving a cloud of black dust to settle before shutting the door. It was a ritual that happened every week and I swear the coalman's face got blacker with each passing week.

The kitchen was very small with wood panelling on the walls that matched the sitting room. Towards the end of the kitchen was a large cold pantry with tiled shelves where milk, bread, eggs, vegetables and various tins, bottles and jars were kept. It was also where our pop, which was delivered weekly by the pop man was kept. Me and my brothers got to choose a bottle each which was a real treat. The idea was that we would share the bottles between us but Robert had a different idea. He always picked a flavour that me and Alfie didn't like, usually dandelion and burdock, which meant that he could have the whole bottle to himself. I think this was the first time I realised that Robert was destined to be a business-man!

Because the kitchen was so small and there was no room for a normal kitchen table Dad designed and made a wooden drop leaf table which he carefully and securely attached to the wall.

To use the table required a little ingenuity and a bit of manoeuvring, you would lift the table leaf up, pull out the 'leg' that would support the leaf and then, like magic, was a small table where you could sit for meals. As it wasn't very big only me and my two brothers Robert and Alfie, were able to sit at the table. There was no space for Mam or Dad so Dad would have his meals on a tray by the fireside often watching the news as he ate. We never really saw Mam eat, I think she just snacked or ate her meals on the move. Even at special times like Christmas this was how we had our meals.

Just off the sitting room were the only two bedrooms in the flat - one for Mam and dad and the other, which had 3 single beds, was shared by me and my two brothers. It was a bit of a squeeze and a squash in our bedroom, and we only had one single wardrobe and a single chest of drawers with three drawers, but somehow, we managed to share in a way that we could each have our own dedicated space where we kept our clothes and toys.

Although the bedroom was small the furnishings were all co-ordinated with the beds having matching quilted nylon bedspreads in shades of orange, brown and yellow with curtains to match.

The bathroom was generous in size with a ceramic sink, metal bath and toilet. Dad tiled the bath wall and the bath panel. The bath was huge and when we were young two of us could easily fit into it at the same time.

We were one of the first families in Chester Close to get a colour TV from Rediffusion, a local TV rental company and I remember, as though it was yesterday, when it arrived. This square box, being carefully carried by two burly men was so huge, well it seemed huge to me. The men carefully positioned the TV in the corner of the sitting room, moving it into a particular angle so that it could be seen wherever you were sat in the room. The men carefully turned on the TV, tuned in 3 stations and then left, happy that everything was working as it should be. Mam, Dad, me and my brothers were so excited. Mam moved a small round table and placed it right next to the TV and covered it with a white embroidered cloth. She then placed our square shaped green telephone on the table.

The telephone was on a 'party line' which meant you shared the line with someone else. It was odd because you could pick up the phone, start to dial a number and then hear someone a couple of doors away talking to someone. If this happened Mam would quickly put the phone down, wait a few minutes and then pick up the receiver again, hold it to her ear and if someone was still talking put it down again. This could happen several times before Mam could actually make a call. Me and my brothers used to find this quite hilarious as Mam would literally drop the phone as though it was possessed and then just look at it as though it was going to chase her around the room which, of course, never happened.

The flats both next door to us and above us were all occupied by different family members or friends and over the years families just seemed to move from one flat to another or from one of the flats into a house. There was a real sense of community with generations of families living and growing up together.

Even though some of the neighbours weren't blood relatives we would still call them Auntie or Uncle as we were all friends, and they really did feel part of our family.

One, 'Auntie Hannah', whose house always smelled like freshly baked brown bread, would make paste eggs every Easter for me and my brothers. Paste eggs are an old British tradition. The tradition involves colouring eggs by wrapping them in onion skins and boiling them until the eggs are hard boiled. The eggs are then eaten over the Easter period.

Another, 'Auntie Lily' who was tiny, would make home-made biscuits and another, 'Auntie Ada', who was married to 'Uncle Eddie', was very kind and quite memorable because she always wore a bright multi-floral frilly apron, or pinny as we called them in the North, that would be tied at them back.

Auntie Ada's house was always spotlessly clean. She was very kind and generous and would knit me a jumper every Christmas with tight cuffs and waist welts. Sometimes she would even buy the wool from the Shetland Isles. The jumpers were really nice and really special and she made them for me right up until my teenage years.

Most of the neighbours in Chester Close were genuinely kind, considerate and supportive and would always look out and help one another. But, as time went by I came to realise that not everyone was always quite who or what they seemed to be.

Go carts & bonnie night

Bonfire

Grandad Alf with Dad Frank

Chapter 5

Grandparents

Grandma and Grandad Castle who were my Dad's parents, my paternal grandparents, moved house and came to live in the adjoining block of flats next to us. My and my brother's bedroom was right next door to theirs with only a wall dividing us. We would often knock on the wall and they would knock back. It became a game and it was great fun! I loved going into their house. Their home was very traditional with a range of mis-matched chairs along with a huge sofa and a mahogany China cabinet that was filled with sparkling glasses.

Grandma was born in Glasgow and was part of a large family having 9 brothers and sisters. After she met Grandad, who was originally from Carlisle, they moved to their first house together in Newcastle.

Grandma was a practising Catholic and her faith was extremely important to her. I remember she had a set of rosary beads and she would often be on her knees by her bedside praying. As she got older and became frail the local Nun's would come to visit her at her home and spend time praying with her.

Grandma was a tall, lean and long woman with red hair that turned grey as the years went by. Her hands were long and wrinkled and one finger bore a single gold wedding band. Her fingers were slender just like her hand and had pointed fingernails which were tarnished a mustardy brown colour from years of smoking cigarettes.

She was so kind-hearted, generous and gentle and she always had time to listen to me, my brothers and cousins. She was always very smart and carried her tall frame very upright when she walked making her look even taller. She would wear lovely clothes, some that she had made herself like the floral dresses and pleated skirts.

When it became acceptable and popular for women to wear trousers she bought some in a dark brown colour. They were made from a synthetic material called crimplene which was textured and sometimes her fingernails would click and catch on the material as her hands rested on her lap. She would always wear the trousers with a fitted blouse or jumper and always a piece of costume jewellery.

Grandma wore pale blue rimmed glasses with pointed corners for most of the time and I would find it really amusing that when she bent forward her glasses often slipped down her nose. She would then use her forefinger to push them back up and every time she did this her small snub nose would give a little twiddly twist that would always make me smile.

Usually, at weekends, Grandma would enjoy a glass of Guinness. She would drink it from a tall, clear glass. I remember it was very dark in colour, almost black, with a creamy coloured foam-like head. Sometimes, when she took a sip, it would leave a small line of cream foam on her upper lip and this would cause her to stick out her tongue, extend it upwards and move it from side to side, licking the cream away. It looked a really lovely drink but once, when she let us taste it, the taste was so bitter it made our faces contort and our shoulders shudder. I vowed never to drink Guinness and I haven't.

She was also quite a character and was the captain of the local Ladies' darts team at the Red Lion pub. As Captain she would lead her team through countless tournaments both local and regional. The team would face fierce opponents but, with her steely determination and unwavering focus the team won many trophies and awards. Grandma was truly proud of the teams' achievements and she would often let me polish the trophies using Brasso. I loved to make them shine and sparkle.

I loved her and we had an unbreakable bond. She was just how you imagine a grandma to be, kind, gentle, caring, empathetic and nothing was ever any bother to her although she was never one to interfere in other people's lives. Her love knew no bounds, extending well beyond just the immediate family. Grandma never had a bad word to say about anyone.

Grandma was a really good cook and made lots of soups using seasonal vegetables that Grandad had grown and she would make lovely traditional meals, and delicious puddings which I loved. Her house always felt and smelt homely. There was always an aroma of freshly baked bread or soups or casseroles. Even now, if I close my eyes I can still smell and almost taste the wonderful aromas-

I remember too, the wonderful earthy smell of Grandad's home-grown tomatoes. He would grow them in big brown plant pots and they would be placed on the windowsill in the sitting room so that the green tomatoes could ripen to a rich red under the rays of the sun.

The tomatoes were quite amazing and we would watch the plants as they slowly developed. They would start small with a strong stem, then leaves would start to sprout and the stem would grow taller with each passing week. Then the flowers would start to open and bloom and as they died away small tomatoes would begin to form where the flowers had been. Eventually the tomatoes would grow to the size of a green golf ball and as the sun shone they would ripen. As soon as they were ripe we would pick them off the branches and eat them straight from the plant, sprinkling salt on them. Delicious!

Saturday in our family was always 'cabbage, tatties and ham' day. We grew up with this and, as far as I'm aware, it's a traditional Scottish dish. Grandma specialised in making it and taught Mam how to make it. It's a simple and easy dish with a clear broth, potatoes, shredded green cabbage and lots of big chunks of boiled ham and lots of salt, pepper and Worcestershire sauce. My Aunt, Uncle and cousins would all go around to Grandma and Grandads on a Saturday to enjoy her speciality meal.

Grandma and Grandad's door was always open so if you were hungry (and me and my brothers were always hungry) then Grandmas was the place to go. There was always a pan of something on the stove and freshly baked bread which Grandma would cut into huge chunks. We would all take a piece and then reach for the big butter knife, with its cream coloured bone handle. We would scrape a huge piece of Lurpak butter and spread it thickly on the bread.

Grandma was always there for us whenever we stumbled or fell, or needed to be supported physically or emotionally. She would always be ready to embrace us with open arms. I remember when I took a tumble off my bike she wiped away my tears and tended to the wounds on my knees, always with a gentle and loving touch.

But it wasn't just her ability to mend our wounds that made her truly special. She possessed an uncanny ability to listen. I mean really listen. She listened to our hopes, dreams and our fears and she would often sit with us for hours on end, her wise old eyes twinkling above her glasses, with genuine interest as we would tell her our stories.

We all thought of Grandma and Grandad's house as an extension of our own home, it was a place where we felt safe and comfortable and could pop in and out of.

Me and my brothers developed a love of darts and there was always a darts board up on a wall somewhere in Grandma's house, usually on the back of a door. The door was always splattered with tiny holes made from lots of stray darts. We all had our own set of darts with colourful "flights" (dart ends) which were almost feather like. Darts was really fun and popular in our family so there was always someone ready and willing to have a game.

Uncle Claude, my Dads brother, lived in the same house as Grandma and Grandad. Generally, he lived their in-between marriages and his many life adventures! He had his own room with a huge wooden bed and when he was not there we would all go to sleep in his room. Robert and Alfie particularly liked to do this and they would have their bath at home, put on their pyjamas, get a tin of tomato soup out of the pantry for their supper and grab their Beano comic then head over to sleep at Grandma's to play darts and have a sleepover.

Grandma always seemed to have time for you. When I was around ten years old she carefully and lovingly showed me how to crochet and how to knit. She had SO much patience. Grandma's passion for knitting and crocheting ignited a spark within me and inspired me to continue to pick up the needles and make my own beautiful creations

Grandad Castle was tall and lean too, just like Grandma, but maybe just an inch or so taller. He was a very laid-back man with oodles of patience and liked nothing more than having his family around him.

Grandad had thinning red hair with a receding hairline. His hair was turning grey but there were still signs of the red hair which were his trade mark in his younger days. He would back comb his hair which had the distinctive smell of the Bryl cream he used to keep his hair in place.

Grandad would get a shave each evening. He would keep his brass mirror and shaving brush hung on the wall by the kitchen sink. Each night he would take off his white shirt and vest and stand bare chested at the kitchen sink to have a shave.

He would soap up his shaving brush, then rub it and swirl it over his cheeks and chin turning his pale cheeks ghost-like and then, with gentle but firm strokes brought the razor from the top of his cheek to his jaw leaving smooth and reddened skin behind. He did this to both of his cheeks and his jaw until there was no soap visible and then splashed his face with water and dried it on his own and very particular towel. It was a routine that never changed until he became too poorly to stand.

I only every remember Grandad wearing a starched white cotton shirt with a Grandad-style neckline, dark heavyweight trousers with turnups at the end of the legs. He kept his trousers from falling down by using a pair of brown coloured elasticated braces with gold buckles that attached to the front and back of the trousers.

Grandad smoked too, just like Grandma. He always had a sort of grey coloured hanky in his pocket which he used on everything except his nose! Maybe that's why it was grey. Resting next to his hanky was a Golden Virginia 'baccy' tin and a small packet of Rizla cigarette papers so he could roll his own cigarettes. He never had a cigarette lighter, just a packet of Swan Vesta matches which he would strike with vigour, making sure the match lit once he had rolled his cigarette.

Grandad was a very practical man and really enjoyed gardening. He would grow all sorts of fruit and vegetables which grandma and other family members would use. I would often pick an apple from the tree or pull a stick of rhubarb straight from the ground and dip it into a cone of sugar - delicious.

Grandad loved his budgies and had many over the years. He would spend many hours teaching the budgies to do different tricks. Some of the tricks were quite amazing.

Peter, one the budgies, was particularly enthusiastic to learn new tricks and was particularly skilled at playing ping pong football - even scoring goals. Peter would also fly from his cage and quietly sit on the side of Grandads dinner plate just waiting to eat any scraps of food that were left.

As well as gardening and training the budgies Grandad loved reading the daily newspaper. He would check the racing results, study the racing form and have small bets on the horses.

In later years Grandad established a local window cleaning business, cleaning windows on the estate. It was a big estate and both Grandad and Rocky were the two window cleaners working the estate, each with their own customers and pitches.

When me and my brothers were quite small we would go around the houses with Grandad collecting money from his customers. It was great fun and Grandad would give us a treat at the end of the collections.

Grandad would always have his ladders chained up at the house to keep them safe but neighbours would regularly ask to borrow them when they'd locked themselves out of the house.

He was a gentle and quiet man and much more of a listener than a talker but he was patient and would share with me stories about his working life. Grandad was always cheerful, thoughtful and reserved and would never have a bad word to say about anyone.

Nana Nell was my maternal grandmother. My Mam's father was a local and very wealthy businessman but he and Nana Nell never married. However, they remained good friends. Some years after Mam was born Nell got married to a man called George. Over the years she and George went on to have 3 more children. I always felt a bit uncomfortable around Nana Nell. She was never very approachable or friendly and didn't show much emotion, either happy or sad. Although, if you were a crook or a gangster then her face would light up and she would become alert, interested and engaged and give her full and undivided attention.

When we were young me and my brothers used to call her Big Nana because she was so big in more ways than one. She was tall, wore big jewellery and had a big personality.

Nana Nell's marriage didn't last and after her divorce she left the West End of Newcastle and moved to a flat near to us. She made her flat very lavish and it was full of every kind of furniture and furnishings you could imagine.

There were expensive ornaments, huge real flower displays, lots of horse figurines and pictures of horses hanging on the walls. In many ways she appeared to live her life as I would imagine gypsies or travellers do. Her purse would always be bulging with notes - monetary notes and all our family knew was that if they needed money they could always go to Nana Nell and she could give them a loan

Not long after she moved house one of her sons, Geordie along with his family, moved into a flat next door to hers.

Appearance and status were important to Nana Nell so she would visit the hairdressers every week for her greying dark bushy hair to be set. She wasn't a particularly attractive woman but she had a tall and imposing frame, exuded confidence and didn't suffer fools gladly. She would generally wear smart skirts and jumpers accessorised with lots of heavy gold jewellery. The fingers on her large, broad hands were full of thick gold rings, 3 were on one finger alone and she would have several thick gold necklaces hanging at different lengths around her neck.

The earrings she wore were large and solid gold. They were so big and so heavy that they made the piercings in her ears stretch downwards.

When she was working she often wore a pink tabard - a sort of overhead apron, which had deep pockets, a place where she could securely and safely keep her purse. She also carried a huge bunch of keys which clinked and clacked when they moved. The keys were attached to a gold horseshoe shaped key ring the size of which I can only liken to that which jailers carry around.

Nana Nell always had money, lots of money, money that no-one really knew how she came to have it. She would regularly place bets on horses, mostly unsuccessful, and, at one stage, she even owned a couple of horses. Such was her love of horses that she went every year to the Appleby Horse Fair where she would make more money by selling riding boots.

Nana Nell was what you would call a wheeler and dealer. It was a skill she had learned during her time working in pubs. She always led a very full social life running several pubs at a time in the West End of Newcastle during the 50's and 60's.

The West End of Newcastle was a tough and very deprived area at that time. It was built around industry and was densely populated by families living in rows and rows of terraced housing. The families were large in size and many were hard-working but it was still an impoverished area and people did what they needed to do to put food on the table and make ends meet.

Nana Nell was definitely a force to be reckoned with and her pubs stood as a bastion of intrigue attracting a colourful clientele that ranged from petty criminals to local gangsters. But, behind her well-dressed demeanour and her ostentatious gold jewellery, a mystery lurked. No-one could quite work out the source of her seemingly endless wealth.

The bustling pubs Nana ran were a constant hub of activity providing refuge for patrons from the harsh realities of their daily lives. Nana could command any room with an air of authority. She had a magnetic and unwavering presence and her heavy gold necklace, rings and earrings would glisten in the dimly lit bars.

It was often whispered among the regulars that Nana Nell had connections to a shadowy underworld and that she rubbed shoulders with some notorious characters. Rumours would also swirl around that she was a mastermind at orchestrating illicit deals and was a trusted confidante to local gangsters.

Despite the whispers she never let slip any hint of her true dealings. Her purse was always bulging with money, a testament to her hidden wealth. Although the origins of her fortune remained shrouded in mystery she was generous to her family and friends and if anyone needed money she was always able to offer them a loan.

After working in the pub trade for a number of years she then worked in the market in Newcastle. The market was full of interesting and colourful characters and Nana Nell thrived in this environment. The market was her stage, she was well known, well informed and well positioned in the hustle and bustle of the city centre market.

She worked in a range of retail units in Newcastle City but in her final working years she was a florist. The Grainger Market was a hive of activity and a real community. All the traders knew each other and the barrow boys would help unload stock for the traders. It was a place for eating, shopping and gossiping.

A lot of ducking ad diving, wheeling and dealing went on too. Stolen goods were bought and sold and Nana Nell, with her bulging purse, was always ready to grab a bargain. She was known to have bought and sold stolen contraband and made herself small profits. She became well known for buying and selling and she was able to forge new relationships with the City's up and coming criminal fraternity and she loved it, she was totally in her element.

As time went on her son Geordie became heavily involved in dubious crimes, and at times, serious, criminal activity. Nana Nell would often protect him and act as an alibi for him or supply the money needed to facilitate criminal activity. She enjoyed and relished being a part of the criminal fraternity as it gave her an importance, power and status. Something that would later come to have terrifying consequences.

Grainger Market Newcastle

Cabbage, Tatties & Ham

Recipe

3 cups of shredded green cabbage

2 large potatoes cut into half

6 cups of stock

Ham joint (steep the night before)

Instructions

1. Soak the ham the night before to remove the salt. Then boil, remove the ham strain the water return to pan add chunks of potatoes, then add shredded green cabbage boil, simmer then shred the ham into it & season with salt and pepper.

2. Put the onions, cabbage and potatoes into a pan

3. Add the stock and ham and season well

4. Bring to the boil and then simmer for 30-40 minutes

Chapter 6

Hot and Bothered

It had been the most amazing summer, *the* most amazing six weeks school holidays. Blue skies and bright sunshine, not to mention the thermometer reaching highs of 80 degrees Fahrenheit which meant children could play outside each and every day from morning until night.

Many of the neighbours in our block would sit outside, men in their string vests and women with their skirts pulled above their knees, catching the sun's rays or seeking shade from the heat. The front doors would be open to let what little air there was circulate around the house. Sometimes we would eat outside with picnic food and chips from the local chippy.

Our family didn't have much money, nobody did, but we didn't need money, we could create our own imaginary world building dens from clothes airers and old sheets or blankets, planning picnics with invisible food, inviting our dolls to join the party. It was all such great fun and we would played out from morning until dark o'clock during the school holidays.

We would pick buttercups and hold them under each other's chins to see who liked butter and we would pick daisies, splitting the stems and joining them together to make long daisy-chain necklaces. We played lots of skipping games, singing along to the rhyming tunes and jumping in and out of the rope. We played with tin cans, the sort that may have contained baked beans. Dad put holes in the sides and attached rope so that you could walk with them. To make them work you would slide each foot on to the top of the tin, grab hold of each of the ropes with your hand and walk, as normally as you could, lifting each foot by pulling upwards on the rope and hopefully you didn't fall over. It was great fun because it meant you were at least six inches taller, and when you walked it sounded as though you were wearing high heels.

We would also pretend to dress up and put lipstick on - the lipstick was made from a red coloured chocolate Smartie that we licked and then spread it around our lips as though we were using a lipstick. We'd then get out our dolls prams and put our babies in the pram, covering them with a blanket to keep them warm, and off we would go taking our 'babies' for a walk and stopping every now and then to comfort them, feed them or adjust their blankets. We didn't have a care in the world and we would play for hours upon hours and never ever got bored.

I remember that we played 'Jazz Bands' and would copy the real jazz bands that competed in local competitions. We made gorgeous band sticks using a broom shank and decorating it with coloured electrician tape and putting an old plastic tomato ketchup squirter, the ones in the shape of a tomato, covered in silver foil on the end to resemble the real Majorettes Mace. The girls were the majorettes and the kazoo players twirling the band stick and the boys were made to be the drummers and we would march around the block.

Me and my friends loved the blue skies and the heat of the summer but Grandma and Mam didn't seem as keen. They regularly complained about how hot it was, how there was no 'air' about and how exhausting the heat was. I remember at one point in August there was so little fresh water that water rationing was brought in. Now that was something I couldn't understand and seemed very odd as I'd only been to the beach the previous week and the sea looked full of water to me!

I told Dad about my confusion and he explained that due to the glorious summer lasting for many weeks there had been very little water-fall so the rivers were drying up which meant there was less water available for homes.

It was the very next day a couple of large wagons drove into the Square and four men, all in dark blue boiler suits, got out of the wagons and starting walking around the pavements looking for - well I'm not sure what they were looking for - but they must have found it as they started digging and lifting paving flags. Once they lifted four flags, they then inserted a long thick pipe which stood about 3-foot-tall, and they fitted the end of the pipe with a tap. The men who were fitting the pipe said it was called a standpipe and it would be where all of the people living in Chester Close would access water for the next couple of weeks.

Me and my brothers thought this was all very exciting and it became quite an adventure to search in the house for a large lidded receptacle that could securely hold water and could be carried to where the standpipe was located. Everyone would wait patiently, in line, until it was their turn to get some water. Some people had large flagons whilst others had bottles or buckets. We had a large flagon that Grandad had once used to make and store his home-brew beer in.

I only went to the standpipe a couple of times but when I did, I quite enjoyed it. Uncle Eddie, one of our neighbours always seemed to be in the queue when I was and I always seemed to be standing next to him.

Uncle Eddie was a very cheery man with a large rotund face, rosy red cheeks and dark curly hair. He worked for the Council and always had some bullets - that's boiled sweets in case you were wondering - and, without saying a word, he would quietly put his hand into his jacket pocket and slip one to me whilst raising a vertical forefinger to his lips and uttering a quiet sshhh indicating that it was our secret and I shouldn't tell anyone. I would quickly take the sweet, and almost silently mouth the words 'thank you' and then popped it in my mouth and quickly sucked and crunched it to make sure that it was all gone before I got back home.

After two weeks of restricted water and numerous trips to the standpipe the weather suddenly, dramatically and rather unexpectedly changed.

The sky turned dark, the brooding clouds loomed overhead and the air felt electric. You could hear the rolling rumbles of thunder in the distance. The rumbling sounds came ever closer, creeping their way towards us and then, with huge flashes and crackles of lightening, the heavens opened.

Down came the rain, it was bouncing off the ground like straight pokers and the paths and roads started glistening like diamonds. The sound of the rushing water filled the air as puddles formed and grew turning the streets into miniature rivers.

I could see Mr. Bull running as fast as his legs would go to take shelter in the doorway of the butcher's shop. I can remember hearing different comments from the grownups. They were saying things like 'We needed this storm to clear the air' and 'The rain is just what the garden needs'.

The storm brought the heatwave to a sudden end but luckily for me and my brothers it was virtually the end of the school holidays. It was only days away before we would be back to the normality of school life.

I started to reflect and thought about the great times me, my brothers and friends had during the 6 weeks summer holidays. I could never have visualised how things would dramatically change over the years ahead and how my life and our family's lives would change forever.

Standpipe in the street

Chapter 7

Sun, Sea and Spam

Today is going to be a great day so I wake up really early and see the pale sun peeping through the edge of the bedroom curtains. Mam is already up and about as I can hear the floorboards creaking and squeaking as she walks around.

Today will be a good day even if it does rain! Nothing is going to spoil today. Dad is taking me, Robert and Alfie to the beach where we'll be meeting my Aunt, Uncle and cousins. As usual, Mam is not coming, she never comes, she always says she is too busy preparing meals or doing housework. It would be nice if Mam came, maybe just once.

I slip out of bed quietly, trying not to wake Robert and Alfie and tip toe out of the bedroom. Mam hears me and shouts "April, come in the kitchen and get the breakfast ready for your Dad and brothers and when you've done that you need to get the picnic ready for the beach".

It always seems to be me that has to make breakfast and tea and it's always me who has to tidy up, clean and go to the shops. Maybe it's me because Mam is preparing me for when I grow up, get married, have my own house and maybe my own children.

I make a start on breakfast and fill the kettle with water, I make a pot of tea in the big brown shiny teapot which I had to use two hands to lift, and then cover it with a red, yellow, green and brown striped tea cosy that Grandma had made. I don't know exactly when she made it as it's the only tea cosy I'd ever known.

Dad always had his tea out of a big white mug. He liked his tea strong with milk and two sugars. Mam would have her tea in a small floral china cup which sat on a plain pink saucer. She always had it medium strength, a sort of mid-brown colour and she didn't take sugar. She always said she was sweet enough! Dad normally had a couple of slices of white bread, that was thickly sliced from a large loaf, then toasted until it was brown and crispy. He loved butter and would spread the toast with lashings of butter. Mam never seemed to eat anything in the mornings. I don't ever recall seeing her have anything in the morning other than her cup of tea.

After making Mam and Dads breakfast I made breakfast for me, Robert and Alfie. Robert and Alfie were now up and out of bed and sitting in the kitchen in their blue striped pyjamas quietly waiting for their breakfast. I never quite understood why they couldn't make their own breakfast because we always had the same thing; cornflakes with milk and a sprinkling of sugar and a slice of bread which was spread with a thin layer of butter and strawberry jam. We would sometimes have a glass of milk but more often than not we didn't bother with a drink because we had milk on our cereal.

With breakfast over it was time to start on the picnic. The first job was making the sandwiches - spam sandwiches. I sliced the bread thinly, spread it with butter and then placed thin slices of spam in the centre, sandwiched the bread together and cut into four pieces.

Next job was the juice. I put some orange squash into a large jug and diluted it with water and then poured the juice into four individual, multi-coloured plastic beakers making sure that I screwed the lids on tightly so we wouldn't have any spillages. Leakages could be disastrous! There was one picnic when the juice had somehow manged to leak onto the sandwiches making them not only soggy but giving them the most peculiar and unpleasant taste imaginable. Yuk!!

Finally, for an extra special treat, I asked Mam if we could take some crisps with us. She turned to look at me and gives me an evil eye but reluctantly agreed to my request. I walked along to the pantry, opened the cupboard door and took out 4 small packets of Smiths crisps. I loved Smiths plain crisps because within each packet was a little twisted piece of blue greaseproof paper that held lots of grains of salt. After opening your packet of crisps, you would carefully search for the blue packet and then untwist the paper and shake the salt onto the crisps. Then, before eating a single crisp, you would grip the top of the packet and vigorously shake the packet to distribute the grains of salt. Only then could you savour the flavour of the crisps– delicious!

I gathered everything together ready for the picnic and then packed the sandwiches, crisps and juice into a small straw shopping bag which had multi-coloured handles and a woven white and yellow daisy on the side. I put a red checked tea towel on the top of the basket to help stop the picnic sliding around.

Dad shouts to us all that the bus is due in an hour so we'd better get a move on. Me, Robert and Alfie all dash to the bathroom and quickly get washed and dressed ready for our trip. It was SO exciting. Mam is making herself look busy but doesn't seem to be doing anything. She's in the kitchen moving clothes from one pile to another. She was concentrating hard but ignoring everything that was going on around her.

Dad reminds us to hurry up because we need to catch the number 34 bus to the beach because we were meeting up with Auntie Jeanie, who is dad's sister, and her husband, Uncle Laurie, and cousins in the car park so we couldn't be late.

I remember that Uncle Laurie had a really nice and very posh blue car. I was very jealous of him having a car and I always wished we had a car. I know going on a bus can be quite an adventure but the journey always seems to take forever.

I started to get excited about the day ahead and then a memory flooded into my head and my stomach started to churn, it was churning with a nervous excitement. Uncle Laurie ..... he would always 'chub us'. I loved Uncle Laurie, he was really lovely, cheerful and funny, always laughing but he enjoyed 'chubbing' us whenever we met. Chubbing took the form of pinching each of our cheeks by using two fingers on each of his hands. The game was to run away before he could chub' us but he always got us and everyone would laugh when each of us were chubbed.

Miraculously the rain that we had the night before stopped and today the sky is a mixture of sun and cloud and feeling a little cool. It's the kind of day where we didn't need to take any raincoats but it was best to have jumpers for Robert and Alfie and a cardigan for me just in case it got a bit chilly. Dad said it was time to go so we said a quick bye to Mam and set off to the bus stop, picnic baskets in hand.

The bus was due at 10.05 am and arrived right on time. After what seemed like hours but it was only 45 minutes we finally arrived at the bus stop close to the beach. The sun was still shining, the skies were blue and the gentle waves glisten as they roll and swish along the water's edge.

Dad guided us from the bus stop over to the car park where Aunty Jeannie and Uncle Laurie and our cousins have already arrived. Uncle Laurie is bent over into the boot of his car trying to reach their picnic basket with its blue gingham cover, blanket, windbreak and a large multi-coloured beach ball which was already inflated. We all stood back from where Uncle Laurie was because we thought he was trying to trick us so that he could chub us. Little Peter who is only 4 is screaming with excitement swinging his bucket and spade in readiness to make sandcastles. Michael is 9 years old and makes a bee-line towards Robert and Alfie.

All nine of us follow Dad and clambered down the sandy slopes to find a nice spot that was not too close to the water's edge and where we could lay out our huge red picnic blanket.

Uncle Laurie had brought a stripy windbreak to protect us all from the gentle breeze and to stop the sand blowing into the drinks and sandwiches. The posts of the windbreak needed to be sunk into the sand so Robert and Michael found a huge stone which Uncle used to tap the posts into the sand. Guess what Uncle Laurie ran up and chubbed both of them. We all screamed with laughter, running away so that he couldn't chub us.

We were all so excited to be at the seaside. I quickly took off my shorts and T-shirt and revealed a green 'quilted' swimming costume. It was a lovely swimming costume, until you went in the water and then it took on a life of its own. The quilted diamond shapes filled with water making all of the sections expand. My brothers said I looked like a huge frog.

I took Peter with my cousin Jane down to the edge of the sea to gather some water to make sandcastles with Alfie. We held hands and gently jumped over the waves as they rolled towards us. Peter loved it and would squeal as he jumped the waves and then ran back towards Jane. Alfie was much more cautious and didn't really like getting wet but we always had a great time.

Dad shouted that it was time for the picnic so we all made our way back and sat down on the red blanket with our legs crossed. We share the sandwiches and crisps. Uncle Laurie had brought some prawns. Dad loved any kind of fish so he picked up a handful of prawns which were sitting in a small blue and white ceramic bowl. The joy on his face when he was eating them was something to behold.

Auntie Jeannie had brought a large flask of tea. She poured the tea into small plastic cups for Dad, Uncle and herself. It was a fantastic picnic with lots of different things to choose from - even strawberries. Dad said we had to sit quietly for half an hour after the picnic otherwise we would be sick. We sat quietly and decided to carve our names into the sand using our fingers. Uncle Laurie took a picture and the adults all thought it was amusing.

We all loved our days at the beach, laughing and feeling totally free to have family time together.

Then, as the tide went out, it was time for whelk picking on the rocks. My Dad absolutely loved any type of seafood so we always went picking Willicks when we were at the seaside. We were all armed with a carrier bag and then set off to the rocks where we rummaged around the rocks, sea wood and rock pools for the brown and black snail shaped Willicks. We rummaged for what seemed like hours but we always managed to at least half fill our carrier bags. Dad would take them home, boil them in a huge pan filled with salty water. When they were cooked dad would put them in bags, salt them and share them out between us. We would each have a pin to pluck out the black 'eye' and green 'snot-like' gel and eat it all. We loved it, absolutely loved it! As I've grown older I just wince at the thought of even touching the Willicks never mind eating them.

The skies started to turn grey and there was a gentle breeze coming from the sea so it was time to go home. We packed everything up, helped Auntie & Uncle Laurie to take the windbreak and blanket back to their car, said our goodbyes and headed for the bus home with our bags of Willicks and rosy red chubbed cheeks.

At the beach

Chapter 8

Mysterious Mutterings

What a fantastic day it had been. Spending time with Dad, Auntie and Uncle and my cousins was just the best thing ever. I'm sure it would have been even better if Mam had come but Mam never, ever, came with us and I could never understand why.

Why wouldn't she want to come and join in with all the fun? I'm sure a day at the beach was a whole lot nicer than a day doing housework. I know if I had a choice I would always choose to go out and have fun rather than stay indoors and do housework.

When we got back to our house we were all still excited but quite tired and hungry. I think I remember someone saying that the sea air makes you hungry. Mam was in the kitchen as usual and was cutting some potatoes up ready for tea.

The boys and I were excitedly telling Mam about our day at the beach and how we'd collected loads of Willicks but she didn't seem at all interested and didn't even make any comment or acknowledge what we were saying she just carried on peeling and cutting potatoes.

Just as we were walking away looking quite dejected she told us to put our swimming costumes into the laundry basket and to make sure that we took our shoes and towels outside and to give them a good shake to get rid of all the sand. She didn't want sand or any mess in the house so we all did exactly as we were told.

Dad went into the kitchen with a big bag full to the brim with the Willicks we had all collected at the beach. Dad washed his hands at the kitchen sink and then started to prepare the Willicks ready for cooking. You could tell from the look on Mams face that she wasn't happy. Mam didn't like Willicks and she didn't like the mess they created or the smell they made but Dad loved them. He loved absolutely any kind of seafood.

After tea and much later that night, around 8pm, the rain was falling really heavily outside, you could actually see it stotting off the ground and bouncing in huge puddles that had formed on the paths and road. Even though it was raining heavily Grandma came across to the house. She was wearing a dark raincoat and a clear plastic hat that was protecting her hair from the rain. Grandma said she had come over with some veg from Grandad's garden. Grandma thought Mam could use the veg for this week's cabbage, tatties and ham which was a scrumptious Saturday tradition.

No sooner had Grandma arrived when Mam called for me, Robert and Alfie. Mam reminded us of the time and said we needed to get bathed and into bed early as we had school the next day. We quickly did as we were told and got bathed and ready for bed. We said goodnight to Mam and Grandma, I gave them a hug and then we all went off to the boy's bedroom. Robert and Alfie were both really tired so after Robert had said his prayers they jumped into bed and were soon fast asleep. But I wasn't really tired.

As soon as the boys were asleep I crept quietly to the lovely new bedroom Dad had built for me.

Dad thought that I was getting too old to be sharing a bedroom with my brothers so during the summer holidays he designed and created a bedroom by converting the veranda area of our house.

Dad was very creative, practical and resourceful and had a great knack for DIY. Dad worked really hard and within a few weeks he had created a completely new room just for me. It was beautiful. It was magnificent. I had my own opening window, the old coalhouse was converted into a walk-in wardrobe, there was a large dressing table with a mirror, a padded stool and single bed. The decorations and furnishing in the room were all co-ordinated in shades of pink and burgundy. I loved it and called it my chocolate box bedroom.

The bedroom became my own little sanctuary where I could retreat and enjoy the calm and tranquillity I needed. I soon moved all of my Sindy dolls from the boys' bedroom into mine but before bed I would often go into the boy's bedroom until Robert had said his prayers and then go off to my bedroom.

I liked school as it was often a distraction from the daily needs and wants of Mam. I was excited about going back to school and wearing my new uniform, especially the smart royal blue knitted jumper that Aunty Ada had lovingly made for me.

I sat on the side of my bed playing with my Sindy dolls and excitedly thinking about meeting up with all my school friends. I was being very quiet but I could, if I listened really hard hear the hushed voices of Mam and Grandma in the living room.

Mam and Grandma both seemed very serious, their voices were deep. their words sharp and both seemed full of emotion. My mind went into overdrive.

I've always been a curious, interested and observant girl and I have a knack of picking up on subtle cues and deciphering them so I tried to analyse what was going on. I wondered if they were talking about me and if I had done something wrong or very wrong or if I had done something to upset someone.

I was anxious and desperate to know more so I crept closer to the bedroom door in the hope that I could hear a little clearer. Most of what they were saying was muffled and pretty much indecipherable so I couldn't make out all of the conversation just bits and pieces of what they were saying but I definitely heard the words ill, hospital and die and it was Mam's voice that spoke those words. Was Mam ill? Who were they really talking about?

As I came to discover, many years later, this was the start of Mams many secrets and lies. This was when I first realised that I was living in a house of secrets. Little did I know that the journey to uncover the truth was just beginning and that I was embarking on an adventure that would require courage, determination, strength and resilience.

I loved and trusted my Mam because she was my Mam and it's a child's natural instinct to love and trust their parents, to look to them for love, care and guidance and for them to provide a sense of security and stability. But, over many years, even decades I came to realise that Mam was not who I thought she was but she was the one who would shape, impact, manipulate and devastate my life, my family's life and the lives of many others.

My Mam's varied and often extreme behaviours together with her incessant need for power and control changed lives forever. She changed them in unimaginable ways and to an extent that we may never know.

Chapter 9

Fearing the Worst

Despite a night with very little sleep I wake up early after a night of tossing and turning in bed, trying to make some sense of what I had heard Mam and Grandma talking about. Did I really hear the words ill, hospital, die or did I imagine it? Was Mam talking about herself or Grandma or Grandad. Maybe she was talking about Dad, Robert, Alfie or another family member or a neighbour. My thoughts were swirling and racing through my head making me almost breathless with the gravity of it all.

I was really fearful that it could be Dad that was ill. Only recently, a matter of weeks ago, Dad's best friend and workmate, Tony, had died after an accident at work. He had fallen from the roof they had been working on. Dad was with him when the accident happened and was so upset. We were all upset.

My Dad and Tony had been friends since childhood and me and my brothers were now friends with Tony's children and we often played together. It was a really sad time for everyone, his family, his friends, his workmates and neighbours and lots of tears were shed. But we were a close community and we all supported each other.

In the aftermath of the accident and the death of Tony I remember feeling really worried that my Dad could fall victim to a similar fate. He worked on roofs so he too could fall off one and die. I became really anxious and the constant worry for his safety and well-being weighed heavily on my mind.

Although the death of Tony was a sad distraction I was still left trying to work out what I had heard Mam and Grandma talking about and what it was really all about. All sorts and everything were going through my mind. Could Mam have been talking about something she had seen on TV or maybe she had seen in a film? Maybe she was reciting something that someone else had told her about someone they knew. It was all extremely worrying, confusing, frightening and really quite terrifying but I knew that I had to find out more about what I had heard.

Initially, I thought long and hard about how I was going to explain the way in which I'd actually overheard what Mam and Grandma had been talking about especially when I was meant to be in bed and asleep as it was school the next day.

Then I thought about forging a plan, a plausible plan that wouldn't cause any suspicion. I decided I could say that I needed to get a glass of water because I had a tickly throat and I was waiting by my bedroom door waiting for grandma to go before I went to the kitchen to get some water because I didn't want to interrupt their discussion. That seemed quite plausible to me.

Mam had a difficult personality and I knew she didn't like being asked questions by anybody and particularly not by me or my brothers. If we asked a question she would often become quite agitated, or aggressive and raise her voice even if you asked a seemingly innocent question. On occasions, she could be quite cruel and would become violent, using anger rather than words to respond so, to ask her about what I had heard, or what I thought I had heard, was always going to be difficult and a challenge that was never going to be easy.

Don't get me wrong, I wasn't frightened of the challenge before me, actually that's not strictly true, I was anxious, a bit nervous and somewhat frightened of how she would respond. Actually, that's not true. I was terrified! I knew, if I was going to ask any kind of question, I would need to plan, with military precision, when, where and how I would do it. But, for now, thoughts needed to turn to the school.

Despite my worries I was keen to go to back to school to meet up with my friends. At least I could escape and concentrate on something other than what was happening at home.

My first day back was great, better than I could have imagined. It was so nice to see my teachers again and I really felt smart in my brand-new uniform even though my new shoes were nipping the back of my heels. I felt sure I would have a blister or two when I took them off.

At the end of the school day I walked slowly home with my friends. I was limping a little because my heels were hurting so much. When I got into our house I immediately sat down and took off my shoes to reveal blood seeping through the left and right heels of my socks. I peeled off my socks and showed Mam my blistered and bloodied heels. She took one look and then gave me a couple of plasters to put on the wounds. She followed this by telling me to put my socks in the laundry basket.

I went to my bedroom and got changed out of my uniform, hanging it up in the wardrobe ready for the next day. I put on my trousers and jumper and then went to the kitchen to help Mam with the chores. Even though I was by Mam's side and helping we didn't have much conversation. She didn't even ask me about my first day back at school. I thought being with Mam in the kitchen might have been a good opportunity to ask her about what I had overhead but I decided to stay quiet, for now.

The whole uncertainty about what I had heard was really troubling me and it was never far from my thoughts. Even when I was at school the worry and uncertainty was never far from my mind.

I started to think that it might be a good idea to talk to Grandma about what I had heard but then, she would probably just say there's nothing to worry about. Children don't need to worry about things that concern adults or she would just tell me to ask Mam.

At least if I asked Mam, the person who actually uttered the words and had the answers to my questions, she could easily explain what it was all about.

So, back to my tentative plan. I knew that when I talked to Mam I would need to show sensitivity, empathy and understanding. I knew I needed to create a safe space where I could explain to her what I thought I had overheard when she had been talking to Grandma on the night before the new school term and that what I had heard had made me really worried.

I reflected on what I was planning to do. Maybe I was worrying about nothing, and those words I had heard were all very innocent. Even if this was the case I was still worried and I needed to know. I really needed to be reassured that my Mam, my Dad and no-one in my family were ill, seriously ill or, worse still, going to die.

Irrationally, I decided it was best *not* to ask Mam. I remember Grandma once saying to me that children should be seen and not heard so I remained quiet and kept my thoughts, worries and anxieties to myself. I would continue to live in a house of secrets.

Chapter 10

The Enigmatic Neighbour

For as long as I can remember, Mam was friendly with Kathy, the sister of a neighbour called Joe who lived in a flat in the next block to us. Joe worked for British Rail and was married to Carole. They had three boys who were similar ages to me, Robert and Alfie.

Kathy regularly came around to our house to see Mam and they would sit and chat over a cup of tea. On one of Kathy's visits, I was in my bedroom enjoying playing with my dolls and the boys were out playing football with their mates.

Suddenly the convivial quiet chat changed and so did the tone of Kathy's voice. It became louder, quite harsh and with a really sharp edge to it.

"Did you know that Carole and the kids have gone away?". Kathy was clearly angry, and I could see her small stout body leaning closer to Mam with her finger pointing towards and almost touching Mam's face.

Mam's eyes quickly turned towards my bedroom where she spied me sitting on the edge of my bed playing with my Sindy dolls. She quickly rose from her chair and strode across the sitting room. With one swift move she shut the bedroom door with such a force that the whole room shook and two of my Sindy dolls fell from the bed and landed on the floor.

I felt quite shaken and didn't really know what was going on. I thought about opening my door and telling them to stop arguing but I thought better of it and stayed safe in my bedroom. I curled up on my bed and covered my ears with both hands to block out the noise.

For the next few minutes, although it seemed like hours to me, their raised voices continued back and forth and the tension between the two of them was palpable. Harsh words were being exchanged and the air was thick with hostility. I really wanted to listen to what they were saying but I was too scared of what I might hear. I didn't want anything else to worry me and prey on my mind, so I had no idea what it was all about.

The next sound I heard was the movement of heavy stomping feet storming out of our house and then the slamming of the front door as they exited. I think the full-blown argument between Mam and Kathy had got to an unbearable point where Kathy couldn't take any more so she left. I gently and quietly opened my bedroom door, just enough so that I could peer out to make sure Mam was okay. Mam looked quite stunned by what had gone on, possibly even looked a little regretful that her friendship with Kathy had in some way been tarnished and was now left hanging by a thread.

I closed my bedroom door and stayed in my bedroom until Mam shouted of me to go to the butchers for some pork chops for Dads tea. Mam seemed agitated, upset and angry so I didn't ask any questions. I didn't say a word, I just took the money and quickly ran off to the butchers.

Only a short while later, when I returned from the butchers I meekly asked Mam "is everything okay?" and asked where Carole and the boys were. Mam still seemed quite angry and certainly not in any mood to tell me anything. She brushed past me, almost knocking me off my feet, and simply said that they had gone away and wouldn't be back any time soon.

I sheepishly started to ask if the boys would still be going to the same school because Robert and Alfie were in the same class as them but I didn't even get a chance to finish the first word as Mam told me, in no uncertain terms, that it was none of my business, to be quiet and to get into my bedroom and tidy my dolls away.

I wondered about Carole and the boys and why they would have left their home so suddenly and why Mam was so certain that they weren't coming back. I'm sure there must have been some logical reason or more than one reason. I'm sure Mam really knew the reason, but she wasn't going to tell me, or Dad or Robert or Alfie. Why was she being so secretive? Why on earth did she need to keep a secret? All I could think was that it must be a seriously big grown up secret.

My curiosity continued and it was only a couple of days after Joe's wife and the boys left that Mam started to make visits to Joe and she would often take me. She fleetingly said that she was helping him because she felt sorry for him. She said that Joe was now on his own and that he was out at work all day and didn't have the time for shopping, cooking or cleaning.

Whenever Mam was making our tea she would almost always make extra for Joe. Mam said it was a kind and neighbourly thing to do. She said that when he came home from a hard day's work he would be able to come home to a nicely prepared meal.

Mam didn't make anything fancy - just simple food. She would make things like; pork chop, egg, chips and spaghetti, and then she would take the prepared food over to his flat, the plate covered with a tea towel. All Joe needed to do when he got home was to boil, bake or fry the food.

I fully accepted what Mam said to me, that she was being neighbourly, and I didn't think too much about this other than Joe was getting more food than we were, and he was getting cake too, generally a peach melba which I thought was a bit unfair. We rarely had cake.

Dad was living at home and working as a roofer at the time when Joe was left on his own. Dad didn't know or have any idea of the increasing time that Mam was spending at Joe's. Mam never gave an explanation about what she was doing for Joe, other than helping a neighbour who was on their own, but the gossip in the neighbourhood was rife.

Neighbours would be on their doorsteps exchanging hushed whispers and speculating about the reason behind Mam's sudden activity at Joe's house. Some believed that Mam had developed a fondness for Joe while others suspected a secret romance was blossoming between the two. Although the gossip continued to swirl and each neighbour added their own imaginative twist to the tale the truth remained a complete mystery within our household and nobody spoke about it. So life just carried on as normal.

After just a few weeks things did start to change and Mam started to do even more for Joe. She would spend more days and longer time in his flat. She would now go several times a week, she would dust, polish and vacuum as well as continuing to prepare meals for him but now it wasn't just one meal a week it was 2-3 meals a week. Conveniently, Dad always seemed to be either at work or out when Mam went to Joe's.

Neighbours continued to gossip and I started to have my own thoughts and concerns about why Mam was spending so much time at Joe's.

Chapter 11

Web of Deceit

Things were changing quickly and after just a couple of weeks Mam was spending more and more time at Joe's. She was doing more domestic chores for him including washing and ironing his clothes and bedding and cleaning his windows. This was all in addition to the general cleaning, bed-making and preparing meals for him that she (or me) was already doing.

It seemed to me that Mam was becoming his very own personal housekeeper. Although I was questioning in my mind why Mam would be helping him so much I suppose I rationalised it all because he was Kathy's brother and he was now living on his own and it was a time when it was generally accepted that women would do housework and look after men because they would be out at work.

As the weeks and months went by Mam was increasingly spending more time at Joe's flat. She was now visiting him several times a week, and usually more than once a day. She would dust, clean, polish and vacuum as well as regularly preparing meals for him but now, instead of just once or twice a week it was three or four times a week. She started to visit him in the evenings too especially when Dad was either working away from home or out at the local club for a drink. I was generally left at home to look after my brothers while Mam was out. She gave me Joe's phone number so that I could ring her if I needed her for something important or urgent but I wasn't to go up to the flat and knock on the door.

Joe was a quiet and unassuming man. A man of few words. There were occasions when I needed to phone Mam when she was at Joes flat to ask when she was coming home. Whenever she answered the phone I could hear Joe in the background shouting "can they not leave you alone for five minutes?" "What do they want?". I would get really worried that I had got Mam into trouble by ringing her. Although Joe was seemingly a quiet man there was clearly another side to him which made me even more wary of him.

I was starting to become resentful of all the responsibility I was being given. I would spend hours trying to work out what was really going on around me and somehow find some reconciliation.

In my head I began to question why Mam would do so much for a neighbour. Why was she spending more time at Joe's, particularly when Dad was away working? I thought about asking Mam why she was doing so much for Joe. But, asking any questions always shrouded me with fear. On the odd occasion, the *very* odd occasion, when I did ask a question to do with family you would clearly see Mam's face contort, her brows would furrow, her eyes would peer directly into yours. She spoke no words but you knew it was best to just walk, or run, away.

For some completely unknown reason questions from me seemed to stir something deep within her as though any response that she might give would provide an insight into her soul and perhaps reveal layers of her character that she may not want you to see. Knowing her reaction left my many questions unspoken.

My relationship with Mam was not an easy one. She was often evasive and her mood could quickly turn from nice to nasty. When I was around her I always felt like I was walking on egg-shells.

Mam always told me that I was special but never explained what she meant or why I was special. She told me that she loved me even though her actions were often emotionally distant and she very rarely showed any physical love. She told me that I was her helper and I needed to stay by her side so that I could help her to look after Joe.

On one particular day, I don't exactly remember when, Mam told me, in a nonchalant and roundabout way, that she hadn't been feeling well for quite a while and doctors had told her that she needed to have a special treatment every Monday evening. The treatment would involve going into hospital from tea-time until around 11pm. every Monday. Mam didn't give any details and wasn't at all clear about what was wrong with her, what the treatment would be, how long it would last or how serious her illness was. Mam told me this devastating news, which came out of the blue, in a completely emotionless and matter-of-fact way.

I was stunned by what I had just been told. My first thoughts were was she going to die. As a child of 11 it was all too much to take in. I was so shocked that I wasn't able to understand or comprehend what I had just been told. My mouth was so dry I couldn't even manage to speak. I was crying, sobbing and so upset.

Mam told me that she was okay and that I shouldn't worry too much or get too upset.

The enormity of what Mam had just told me made my head feel as though it was going to explode and I felt utterly and physically sick.

What if my Mam, *my* Mam, is going to die.

All I could think about was if she died then I wanted to die too because, despite her faults, I couldn't live without her. I loved her so much and I knew in my heart that she loved me too.

Once I had calmed down a little I began to put two and two together and wondered if the conversation I had overheard between her and Grandma all those months ago was actually them talking about Mam's illness. Things now seemed as though they were making some sort of sense.

I knew I needed to know more about Mams illness. I *wante*d to know more, I *needed* to know more. What was really wrong with Mam, was she going to get better or was it terminal. I had hundreds of questions going through my head and desperately needed her to give me the answers and the reassurance I craved.

Mam gave me very limited information about her illness and no details other than she needed to go to hospital to have 'kidney treatment'. She said she would be going on a kidney machine to help clean her blood. I remember feeling quite scared, confused and worried and thought that maybe Mam wasn't telling me much because she wanted to protect me from worrying. I remember thinking she was being really caring and thoughtful and that she was such a good Mam to minimise the impact of her illness so as not to worry me or my brothers.

From that day forward Mam involved me in all aspects of her daily life and I was constantly by her side. I happily accepted helping her with all of the tasks she wanted me to do because I loved her and I would do whatever was needed to help because she was my Mam and she was ill.

On that first Monday night when Mam went off to hospital for treatment I was left to make the tea for me, both of my brothers AND Joe. Dad was working away so it was all left to me.

Me and the boys were having sausage, chips and spaghetti and Joe was having the same but with an egg. I prepared our tea and then Joe's. I was keeping my eye on the time as Mam told me I couldn't be late in getting Joe's tea to him.

I put everything on a tray and grabbed the key to his flat. I carried the tray with sausage, egg, chips and spaghetti out of our flat and up the stairs to his flat. I laid the tray, covered by a tea towel, on the kitchen table ready for him to cook when he got home from work. I was so relieved and pleased that he was still at work. I quickly ran out of the flat, firmly shutting the door behind me and ran back downstairs to our flat and watched some TV with my brothers.

Later that evening Grandma came around to make sure we all got washed and into bed at a sensible time. Grandma relaxed back into the armchair and watched Z Cars on the television whilst she waited for Mam to return home from the hospital in an ambulance.

Mam had told me that when her treatment was completed, and as it was late in the evening, an ambulance would bring her home. I was so worried about Mam and how she would be feeling after the treatment that I couldn't go to sleep until I knew that she was safely home.

I heard a key turn in the front door. It must be Mam! I immediately looked out of the bedroom window. It was a clear bright night with dozens of stars twinkling in the sky. I looked up and down the street but I couldn't see or hear any sign of an ambulance which I thought was very strange.

What I could hear was Mam's voice and she sounded quite happy and cheerful as she chatted to Grandma. Maybe things aren't as serious or as bad as I was imagining. Maybe the treatment wasn't as bad as I had thought. I felt a huge sense of relief as I snuggled down into my bed and quickly fell asleep.

Next morning, I woke up feeling quite bright despite my late night. Everything in the house was just as normal, and Mam didn't seem any different either.

I asked her "are you ok? Do you feel better?"

Mam didn't answer, she just ignored me and my question as she often did. I was pleased that Mam was at home and relieved that she looked happy and well so maybe I'd been upsetting myself and worrying unnecessarily.

A few moments later, and even though Mam didn't answer my question she did have a question for me. Her voice was clear and firm. "Why didn't you put Joe's peach melba cake on the tray like I told you to do?" I thought momentarily. I'd completely forgotten about the cake. "Sorry Mam, I completely forgot about it, I'll never forget again, I promise".

The question Mam had asked made me think. How could Mam possibly know that I didn't put the cake on Joe's tray. I considered possible explanations - maybe she spoke to Joe when he was on his way to work this morning, maybe Joe had phoned last night asking where his cake was although I didn't recollect hearing the phone ring Anyway, there was no time to give it much more thought because it was almost time to leave for school,

On the Wednesday morning Mam told me that I wasn't going to school but I mustn't tell my brothers. She told me I would be staying at home to help her with the daily chores. She told me to get dressed in my school uniform so that my brothers wouldn't realise that I wasn't actually going to school and I had to pretend that everything was normal. She then told me to pretend to leave for school but instead to hide on the landing above our flat until my brothers went off to school and were completely out of sight.

As soon as my brothers had gone I returned to our flat and quickly changed out of my school uniform. Shortly afterwards I went with Mam across to Joe's flat. Mam told me to tidy Joe's bedroom, to open the curtains to let some light in and to make his bed. I didn't feel very comfortable about doing this but I did as I was told.

I flung open the bedroom curtains to let the bright sunny light in and, as I turned around towards the bed the first thing I saw was a tall pile of shabby looking, well -thumbed and explicit adult magazines all with torn pages and curled edges. They were laid just by the side of the bed and sort of strewn across the floor as though they had been in a pile that had been knocked over. I shuddered with disgust! I'd never seen anything like them before and I'm absolutely certain that I never want to see anything like them again.

My face flushed with embarrassment and discomfort as I beckoned Mam over to the side of the bed and pointed at the magazines on the floor. Mam's reaction, unlike mine, was calm. She was totally unperturbed by what was in front of her and firmly told me to gather them altogether, stack them into a neat pile and put them back into the wardrobe. I did exactly what I was told to do but as I opened the wardrobe doors I was faced with yet another huge pile of rude magazines.

Touching those magazines made me feel very, very uncomfortable and dirty. I was consumed with an overwhelming urgency to wash and scrub my hands - which I did, as soon as I could, and several times!

I found it odd and quite disturbing that Mam was completely uninterested in what I had found on the floor in Joe's flat and didn't seem to think it was abnormal in anyway to be harbouring such explicit magazines. She showed no emotion and simply continued with dusting and polishing the furniture as though nothing had happened.

Joe didn't have much furniture or furnishings in his flat. The rooms were all very minimalistic but one thing I did notice was that the sofa and a corner table seemed very, very familiar. They were familiar! They were familiar because they were the exact ones we had in our house only weeks before we got our new ones.

Mam had hounded Dad for months to get a new sofa and a new table for the TV. There were arguments galore night after night until eventually she wore Dad down and got what she wanted. We never knew where the old sofa went, or the table, we weren't really interested, but we do now. Another secret.

After a couple of hours Mam was happy that Joe's flat looked spic and span so we closed the door, locked up and went back down to our own flat where we started tidying, cleaning and polishing all over again.

After we had finished the second round of cleaning and tidying Mam said we needed to go over to the shops to get something for our teas. We went to the butchers first and Mr. Briggs, the owner of the butchers' shop, looked at me from head to foot and asked why I wasn't at school. I kept quiet, I didn't know what to say but Mam quickly interrupted any hesitation and told Mr. Briggs that I was off school for the whole day because I had a poorly tummy. Mam said she was hopeful that I would recover quickly and be back to school the next day. Another lie!

My absences from school became a regular occurrence. Mam would keep me off to be with her to help her with her and Joe's household chores. It would even happen when my Dad was at home or working in this country.

There were many, many times when I had to take Joe's tea over to his flat. I always tried not to drop it as I walked through the dark block of flats. The particular block that Joe lived in was not the nicest and, worse still, there was a very weird man who lived in the bottom flat. I was really scared of him so I would quickly run past his door and up the stone steps to Joe's flat. All whilst carrying a tray of food which usually contained eggs!

Once at Joe's flat I would gently put the key into the lock and slowly open the door, hoping that Joe was still at work. I then placed the tray on the bench and set out the food ready to be cooked. My next tasks were to vacuum, make the bed, wash the dishes and put the rude magazines away. After this I quickly returned home, relieved that I had done what I needed to do. Mam was happy that I was doing as she wanted but was always insistent that I was never to tell Dad!

As a child I spent a lot of time by Mam's side. I lived much of my childhood around adults so I was exposed to many adult conversations. I would hear lots of unsavoury gossip. I witnessed lots of adult interactions and behaviours which may have even been illegal or bordering on petty or serious criminality. There was always some sort of drama or crisis happening and which often involved members of my Mam's family.

Mam's family were completely different to Dad's family. They always seemed to be fighting, arguing and there were fallings out between them. There never seemed to be any loyalty between them.

Even as a child I recognised that my Mam was very different to my friend's Mams. My Mam seemed to have a certain knack of using her warm smile and caring demeanour to engage with people and to quickly gain their trust. She was very skilful at connecting with people and exploiting their vulnerabilities.

Mam was cunning but still able to charm people, young and old, with her outgoing and bubbly personality. She loved and craved attention. Her focus was always to build a close friendship with people and, once established, she would create a dependency on her.

She became very popular with neighbours, often doing errands or lifting their spirits when they were feeling down. But what friends and neighbours didn't realise was that she was manipulating and controlling them in ways that they didn't even realise.

As I grew older, and to my cost, my Mam's secrets, lies, power and control were something that impacted me too but in a more sinister way. Mam's lying was really emotional abuse. There was also physical abuse. This abuse affected my trust, my confidence, my self-esteem, my mental health and has influenced my whole life.

My School in 1975

Chapter 12

School and Skulduggery

I really enjoyed school and, amazingly, academically, I did really well despite my poor attendance record (caused by Mam). My brothers did well too. I excelled at athletics whilst my brothers excelled in football. The boys were so talented that they were both scouted for football trials at Nottingham Forest football club.

Because of my talent for sport and my keen interest in dance I really thought that one day I might become an athlete or a ballet dancer. Sadly, this was an ambition I was never able to achieve because of Mam's illness. I was never able to go to any out of school activities like Brownies or ballet because I had to do household chores and look after my brothers and Joe.

I look back on my schooldays with fondness. I particularly enjoyed my primary and middle school, I loved my teachers and when I think back, I admire how committed and attentive they were and how keen they were for us all to do well.

When I was young the class sizes were quite small and had both girls and boys. I had a large circle of friends and I still remain friends and keep in contact with some of my middle school friends to this day.

Friday night was when I would meet up with my friends and we would go to the local Youth Club which was held in the Methodist Church. We would play cards, dominoes, badminton and snooker. There was even a TV room and a dressing-up cupboard but, best of all was the tuck shop which was run by two old couples called Mr. and Mrs Fletcher and Mr and Mrs Wilson. They were church-goers and were very patient and tolerant with us teenagers but I think they enjoyed running the tuck shop just as much as we enjoyed spending our money on sweets.

Dad knew I went to the youth club and he would give me money to buy sweets and drinks. He would always put his family first and do his best for me and my brothers.

For many years Dad had been interested in moving our family to Canada. He thought Mam, me and my brothers would have a better quality and healthier lifestyle living in Canada. He and Mam had talked for a long time about us all moving to Canada and Mam had seemed really keen on the idea until very recently, when she turned against it and started dismissing the sheer thought of moving.

I don't know what or who changed her mind but it caused dreadful arguments. Dad was really frustrated and had many mixed emotions. Mam refused to offer up any reasons or any explanation for her change of heart. Understandably Dad was frustrated at the situation. The arguments continued and became more intense and were happening more regularly. No matter what Dad said or how much me and my brothers pleaded with Mam she was absolutely determined that the family would not move to Canada. As usual, she got her way.

The tension in our house was almost unbearable and I was disappointed and frustrated that any hopes of emigrating to Canada had now been completely and utterly dashed. I think Dad was so disappointed that he needed some space to reflect on what had happened so he started to work away from home again.

Mam was pleased and relieved that Dad was going to be working away because she was always at her happiest when he was away from home. The atmosphere in the house was always a little brighter although she would often take this opportunity to spin a web of lies about Dad in a bid to distance us from him.

Mam would start suggesting things to us like Dad wanted to take us away from our family and our friends, he wanted to isolate us because he was selfish and only thought about himself. She would tell us that he didn't really care about us or what the family needed or wanted.

I loved my Mam and my Dad and I didn't want to take sides but it seemed to me that Mam, somehow or other, was going to make us take her side. It made me think about her behaviours. It was Mam who always managed to stop the family enjoying themselves. She stopped us from going on holiday because of her illness and her regular need for dialysis. She would take a selection of pills because me and my brothers were annoying her and then take to her bed for days. She was the one who stopped me from having a normal childhood because she said she needed to have regular dialysis treatment. It was Mam who wouldn't join in with the rest of the family to go on day trips for no good reason. And now, she wouldn't agree to emigrate to Canada for a better life.

It seemed to me like Mam had made it her life's work to make life dull, difficult, awkward or miserable but I never thought this was deliberate. I accepted that it was because she was ill. I never saw it as unfair, I just did what I had to do to help her and to try and make things as easy as possible for my Dad and brothers.

It was becoming clear that Mam was slowly beginning a manipulative process of turning us all against Dad and at the same time she was grinding Dad down and eroding his personality in order that his relationship with us would deteriorate and ultimately collapse.

Mam was skilled and very clever at hatching plans although her plan to turn me and my brothers against Dad and to make sure that the family didn't emigrate to Canada was going to be a challenge. What she would hatch nobody knew, but her plan, or series of plans, came to have devastating consequences which impacted us all to our very core.

Dad had left the house to work in another part of the country and wouldn't be back until the end of the week. I could see Mam was in the kitchen when I noticed that she appeared to deliberately break a glass. I was in the sitting room and decided not to get involved but just sat and watched Mam as she dealt with the broken glass. She carefully picked up the broken pieces from the floor and put them onto a tea towel which was draped over the wooden bench.

I watched as Mam pounded and ground the broken bits of glass into tiny, almost powder-like, pieces using the end of a large wooden rolling pin. She then gathered the powdered pieces together by folding the tea towel in half to form a sort of shute which she then gently shook and encouraged the powdered glass to gently slide into a small jar. I wondered what on earth she was doing and I couldn't even begin to hazard a guess as to why she was doing it although I didn't have to wait too long before I found out.

Although it was only Tuesday, Mam went over to the butchers and bought a piece of rump steak ready for when dad came home on Friday. Even the butcher Mr. Briggs was surprised. Not many people can afford to eat rump steak mid-week.

Dad loved fish more than anything but a nicely cooked piece of rump steak was his next favourite. When Mam returned from the butchers I watched her as she put the steak, still in its paper bag, in the airing cupboard. Now, the airing cupboard is often very warm, so why, I thought, would you put a steak in there? I'm no cook so maybe there's a perfectly good explanation like making it more tender. I didn't know why she was putting it in the airing cupboard but I wasn't about to ask why either - it seemed like a very odd thing to do.

Whilst Dad was away Mam continued with her regular routine of visiting Joe's house tidying, cleaning and making meals for him except on Mondays of course, when she was having dialysis.

I started to really resent Mondays because I had to make the tea for me, Robert, Alfie and Joe. I'd always try to get Joe's tea made and taken up to his flat before he came home. I never wanted to be alone with him in his flat.

When Dad returned home on the Friday evening we were all delighted to see him, even Mam (strangely). Mam told Dad that she had got him some rump steak which she would serve with an egg and some chips. Dad's face was beaming. I loved it when Dad was happy and smiling, his blue eyes sparkled and he would look so handsome.

Mam cooked the steak which had, remember, been in the airing cupboard for several days and placed it on the plate together with a fried egg and a pile of chips. She then poured a bottle of beer into a large glass and added the glass powder, giving it a quick stir. She put the plate of food and the beer on a tray and took it through to the sitting room where Dad was settled comfortably in his armchair. Dad slowly ate the meal, appearing to enjoy every bit and completely clearing his plate. He finished off his beer declaring the meal and the beer absolutely delicious.

So, I thought, I've learned something new. Storing steak in an airing cupboard for several days and putting powdered glass into beer must add flavour and texture. *Warning – don't try this at home!*

The next morning, Saturday, Dad was different, he was very distant with me, Robert and Alfie. We all couldn't understand why because he had been so happy the night before and Mam was happy too. Maybe he and

Mam had argued again or maybe Mam was wanting more money to waste on things we didn't need or maybe he wasn't feeling too well because of the new way of storing the steak or was it the added flavour to the beer that didn't agree with him. Whatever the reason it was a very, very miserable Saturday.

By teatime Dad had started to perk up a bit and he got himself washed and dressed ready to go to the club for a pint or two with his friends.

Dad always had the same routine before he went out. He would get the boot polish out of the cupboard, clothes out of the wardrobe. Dad would polish his shoes until they gleamed and you could almost see your face reflected in the toe caps. He would take his jacket off the wooden hanger and firmly brush the jacket in strong downward movements removing any tiny flecks or threads. He always looked very clean, tidy and smart.

We always had a roast dinner on a Sunday which I loved. Mam would plate up a dinner for Dad to have when he returned from the club.

Dad only went out for a couple of hours but during that time Mam always went out too. She went to Joe's flat. She told us she was going to wash his dishes and do his ironing. It seemed an exceptionally kind and generous thing to do but she had been doing it for so long we never questioned her.

Mam would always make sure she was back home well before Dad came back from the club. I'm sure Dad knew nothing about her visits to Joe's.

Dad was a creature of habit and always had the same routine on a Sunday afternoon. Dad would go to the club for a few hours, play Bingo and then come home, hang up his jacket by the side of the bed, take off his shoes and slip into bed for a snooze which usually lasted a couple of hours.

I remember that when I was a small child and when Dad returned home on a Sunday afternoon, my Mam would often tell me to sneak into their bedroom and crawl to the side of the bed where Dad would put his jacket. She told me to take some money out of his wallet, crawl out of the room and give the money to her.

At the time, Mam made it seem like a fun thing to do, but I didn't like doing it. It felt wrong. It felt like stealing. Many years later Dad told me that he knew the money was being taken from his wallet and he knew I did it but he also knew that it was Mam who was behind it so, not wanting to cause an argument, he kept quiet and never said anything.

Steak, chips and beer with a sprinkling of powdered glass

Chapter 13

Suspicions

Growing up wasn't easy as I became more and more suspicious about the kind of lifestyle Mam was leading. I was trying to balance having a normal childhood alongside being a carer for Mam and having domestic responsibilities which would normally be carried out by adults. On reflection I suppose I was trying to keep everyone happy, my brothers, my Dad and my Mam who was, after all, seriously ill.

Because of Mam's constant manipulation my Dad was becoming more and more isolated from us. He stopped making efforts to engage with us and stopped trying to appease Mam. Mam was now in control and in charge of everyone and everything!

She now needed dialysis twice a week - on Mondays and Thursdays. Her life, and mine, was becoming defined by the twice-weekly routine of hospital visits. I was feeling really unhappy and unsettled. I felt resentful at having to help out on *another* day, particularly as that day was Thursday. Thursday night was one of my favourites. Thursday was Top of the Pops night on the TV and I loved it. Now I would have to miss it because I would have to make tea for me, my brothers and Joe and then take it across to his flat and then there was the washing up to do! I couldn't help thinking that it was strange that Mam's dialysis treatments were only at night. Why were they not during the day? Another unspoken question.

As the weeks went by I was constantly at Mam's beck and call. Now that she was having dialysis twice a week I couldn't challenge her about anything because, after all, as she regularly told me, she was ill and could die. Mam was spending more time in bed so that meant there was more for me to do. Things were getting worse and there didn't seem any prospect that things would improve any time soon.

It was one Thursday night when I was around 11 years old that our dog, Mac, bit me on my leg. Mac was a German Shepherd and he was big but really friendly. Sometimes he got a bit over-excited and this was one of those occasions. I ran over to Grandma's to show her what had happened and Grandma told me to ring the hospital to speak to Mam. I did as Grandma told me and I rang the hospital. My stomach was doing cartwheels but I nervously explained that my name was April Castle and that I was 11 years old and that our dog had bitten me and I needed to speak to my Mam who was in that hospital having kidney dialysis treatment. I gave them her full name and address and post code.

After a long, nervous and anxious wait the person on the other end of the phone at the hospital told me that they had fully checked their records and that there was no one of that name or address listed as having dialysis that day or any other day. In fact, there were no medical records of that name and address in the hospital at all.

Shocked and bewildered, I thanked them and put the phone down. This was the first time I realised that maybe Mam was lying about being ill. But why would she lie about something so serious.

I told Grandma exactly what the hospital had said on the phone. I looked right at Grandma and her face had a look of resignation. She took a large intake of breath, gave out a loud sigh and said that I needed to ask Mam about it when I got up the next morning. I wondered if Grandma knew something about the hospital being unable to find any information about Mam but she wasn't telling me to protect me.

I remember feeling quite confused and thinking that if Mam was lying about being ill then that was a good thing because that meant she was not going to die. But then my thoughts turned to anger. How could she be so awful and wicked to tell such a lie, a lie that had massive consequences and that impacted our daily family life and the lives of those who were close to us.

My thoughts were conflicted and weighed heavy on my mind but I still did not tell anyone! I still couldn't share my thoughts. I really wanted to believe Mam, I honestly did, because the alternative was just too painful to think about. I'm sure she loved us more than anything and the thought that she could be lying to me and to all of us was just too much to contemplate.

I went to bed that night and my mind was searching for explanations, answers to my questions or any clues that could help me resolve my anxieties. On the one hand she was a good Mam, we had a lovely home, she bought us things, she gave us money, we had nice food and on the other hand she could be cruel – physically and verbally cruel to me and my brothers and she would argue and fight with Dad, always wanting money and her own way.

Somehow Mam had a knack of convincing us that she was always doing her best for us and she did really put a lot of effort into making sure we had everything, that is everything that she had decided was needed. She never showed any real interest in us or praised us for any of our personal or school achievements such as our school reports or sporting achievements.

Mam always tried to make Christmas special for us when we were children and we always spent it at home. We had a really glamorous Christmas tree with lots of beautiful decorations and treats hanging from the branches. We would wake up on Christmas morning to find all our presents carefully set out in the living room. We always received the latest toys and gadgets and no expense was spared. Our stockings would be full of fruits and nuts.

We all enjoyed a very traditional family Christmas dinner with freshly cooked turkey and all the trimmings. Mam always seemed as though she couldn't settle, she couldn't relax until she had sneaked out to take Joe his Christmas dinner without Dad knowing.

The next morning, I decided to ask Mam a few questions about the dialysis treatment to try to make some sense of what the hospital had said so, the next day, I asked Mam "what happens when you go to hospital Mam and when you have your kidney treatment?" She looked straight into my eyes and, with the index finger of her right hand pointed to a small scar on the front of her leg and said "this is where they connect the kidney machine ". My heart sank, so it must be true, she must be ill, the hospital must have made a mistake. Mam is ill and she could still die.

For the first time Mam told me in brief that the kidney machine took all of her blood out of her body and cleaned it and then pumped it back in again as her kidneys were not working properly. This was the first detailed conversation that I had with Mam and it made me want to believe what she told me.

I spent a lot of time thinking about what the hospital had said and how Mam showed me the scar on her leg and I found it incredibly difficult to make any sense of it. How could the hospital be so wrong? Why would Mam lie?

As time went by my mind became more and more tormented. I kept on thinking more and more about Mam's illness and about the regular and increasing help she was giving to Joe. I recalled that there were a few occasions when my Dad was working away and when it was not one of the Kidney dialysis treatment nights but my Mam still went out.

Usually Grandma would come over and babysit if Mam went out but, on this occasion, Mam had arranged for a different babysitter. Mam was normally a plain dresser and never wore high fashion clothes or even makeup but when she went out on these night-outs it was very different. She was different.

I was completely shocked when I saw Mam come out of her bedroom wearing a skin-tight blue trouser suit, matching handbag and white block 6" high heels. Her face was made up with foundation, blue sparkly eyeshadow and bright lipstick. The smell of the perfume was strong and sweet and the heavy gold jewellery was just like what Nana Nell would wear, perhaps she had borrowed it from Nana Nell. I really could not believe my eyes, Mam did look absolutely gorgeous but almost unrecognisable. I'd never seen her look like that before and I'd never seen those clothes or shoes before in her wardrobe or in the house. I wondered if she kept them at Joe's or Joe had bought them for her.

I remember that on one particular Monday, when Mam was having her dialysis session, I had to clean Joes flat so I decided to take a little look around the flat to see if I could find any clues of Mam staying there. I looked for items such as clothes or shoes. I looked everywhere but I couldn't find any clues about clothes but I did find a photograph of Mam looking very, very glamorous and really happy. In fact, the happiest I've ever seen her. She was stood by the bar in a pub that I didn't recognise with a drink in her hand. She was all dressed-up with makeup on and bedecked in jewellery.

The photo aroused my suspicions and my mind was in turmoil and again whirling with a series of questions. What was the photo doing in Joe's flat? Where was the photo taken? What was Mam doing in a pub? Why was she dressed up in more clothes that I'd ever seen before? Why was Mam drinking? I knew it was a recent photo because Mam was wearing the glasses she got less than two years ago.

Mam never wanted to go to a pub. Mam never wanted to go anywhere with us. Dad had often asked Mam to go to the local pub or club with him but she always, always, refused saying she couldn't drink because of the dialysis treatment. But there she was, in this photo, kept in Joe's flat, happy as Larry in a pub, all dressed up and with a glass in her hand!

Another occasion that aroused my suspicions was when Alfie had to go into hospital for a minor operation. It was the same hospital where Mam had her dialysis treatment. Mam, me and Robert went to visit Alfie at the hospital, Dad was working away at the time. We arrived at the hospital a good twenty minutes before visiting time.

We were all just standing around in the hospital corridor when I noticed a map of the hospital pinned on a wall. We were all quite bored so we started to look at the map and Mam pointed to an area on the map where she said she went for her dialysis treatment. I really wanted to see where Mam was going twice a week so I asked Mam "can we go along and just have a look at where you have your dialysis please". Mam responded angrily and said brusquely "no" I pleaded with her just to let us walk along to where the dialysis ward was just so we could have a quick look at where she was spending so much time. We didn't want to go into the ward, just to see where it was but she said "no, absolutely not". This made me wonder and made me even more suspicious. Might she be lying about her illness?

It was really hard to carry on with any sort of normal life when, at the back of your mind, you didn't know whether your Mam was going to live or die or whether she was telling the truth or lying. I became very anxious about what was going on around me but I had no-one to talk to. I couldn't talk to Mam because she would only get angry if I asked any sort of questions and I knew, to my cost, that she wasn't afraid of physically punishing me or my brothers. I couldn't ask Dad as he was working away for most of the time and it was just accepted that Dad was not to know. My brothers were totally dis-interested or perhaps they just didn't want to talk about it or, as long as their tea was on the table, they were happy.

Around this time Joe's and Mam's friendship was becoming more open and he was 'formally' introduced to us as a friendly neighbour. He often came to the flat when Dad was not around and both he and Mam would spend time laughing and talking together. During the summer he would sometimes take me, my brothers and Mam for a ride in his car. We didn't have a car so it was quite exciting especially when we went for a drive along the coastline.

We would often follow the same route along the North East coast line. We never got out of the car, we just gazed out of the windows at the rolling waves of the sea. The drives usually happened during the summer evening and when Dad was working away from home. There was a certain point on the route where there was a crossroads with traffic lights and the lights were always on red so Joe would stop the car. While we were sat at the lights we always admired a small row of big, grand houses. We thought they were very posh houses.

There was one particular house which had a huge shiny black door, decorative arched canopy and pillars at the side. I would look at the house and wonder who could live there and how rich they must be to live in such a grand house. Every time we went past it my curiosity and admiration grew until one day, as we passed the house Mam said "I can book that house for a holiday, it's a holiday home for kidney patients". I was so excited and my brothers were SO excited and we begged Mam to book the house for a holiday. Mam answered firmly saying "Let's see, I will ask the nurses at the hospital". I could hardly contain my excitement, the thought of staying in the posh house with huge windows that looked out to the sea was amazing. Weeks went by and we lived in the hope that the nurses would let us stay there. We never got an answer, we never stayed there.

Mam was always happy being out in the car with Joe. Dad never knew!

I loved my Grandma and would often talk with her but I knew if I asked her about anything to do with Mam she would just say "ask your Mam". I couldn't talk to my friends because they all liked Mam. She would charm them, give them gifts as a way of buying their loyalty and, truthfully, I struggled to work out how Mam was behaving and what was true and what was lies.

As the weeks and months went by I continued with what had become a weekly routine of going to school for some of the time, helping Mam with different household jobs, cleaning and cooking when Mam had her dialysis treatment until one day Mam said that she had received a phone call from the hospital telling her that a suitable kidney had been donated and that she could have a kidney transplant. She was told to pack a bag and to wait for another phone call advising her to go to hospital. So, it was true after all, she really is ill and this transplant might save her life.

There aren't enough words to explain just how excited we were, but equally how worried me and Robert were. We knew the operation could save Mam's life but we also knew it would be a serious and major operation and that she could die.

Our hearts were pounding and we were jumping around with sheer excitement. All we could think about was that Mam wouldn't have to go to hospital anymore and that she wasn't going to die. The excitement and the relief we felt were palpable. Robert and me went into Mams bedroom where she was packing a few bits and pieces into a small holdall and we both knelt by her bed and prayed. We prayed and we prayed "Please God, let there be a kidney for Mam and let there be a match so that she can be better".

I was really surprised that Mam seemed unflustered and very relaxed. I knew there was a possibility that having the operation would massively improve her health and change her quality of life forever but Mam showed no emotions whatsoever. She didn't even acknowledge our emotions and how excited, but worried we were. Mam calmly continued to pack her bag with the things she needed for hospital. When she finished packing she put the bag on the floor next to the bed, slowly walked into the kitchen, made a cup of tea, took the tea into the living room, picked up a magazine, sat down and serenely took sips from the cup, ignoring anything and everything around her including us.

The day passed slowly as the minutes and the hours slowly went by. Robert and me became more and more despondent wondering when and if the call would come. The TV was on, really just as a distraction because we weren't really watching it, we didn't really speak to each other either, we just exchanged an occasional but exasperated glance. As children we didn't know what to say, how to start a conversation with Mam and Mam was just being her 'normal' self seemingly uninterested in what was about to happen. In fact, Mam continued doing what she always did, even preparing the food for Joe's tea and taking it up to his flat. She seemed oblivious to the enormity of the difference a kidney transplant could make and she was calm too, unnaturally calm.

We waited and we waited but the phone never rang and the call from the hospital never came. It quickly dawned on us that the kidney transplant was not going to happen, not this time. This kidney mustn't have been a match. Me and Robert were absolutely devastated and distraught. Robert led our prayers again, we were both kneeling by his bed and he thanked God and asked that the next kidney be a match for Mam.

Mam was very calm, remained completely composed and showed no emotion whatsoever. Somehow, she seemed to know that the call was never going to come and simply said to us, 'never mind'.

I felt very cheated... like the first Christmas in my new chocolate box bedroom and my present that year had been a black and white portable TV. I went to my room to watch the wizard of OZ, for the very first time and I loved it so much, I so wanted to be Dorothy, and to be whisked away. Then the next time I watched the film, I watched it in the living room on the large coloured TV. I was stunned and delighted and so happy to see that when Dorothy landed in OZ and everything turned to beautiful colour. It was simply amazing and with my childhood innocence I knew I would have had that similar amazing feeling if Mam had got her new kidney. I then realised Robert had been praying to God for "magic to happen". Grandma once told us that we should not ask God for things like a new bike because God was not magic and could not give new bikes. Robert and I worried that asking for a new kidney was just like asking for a new bike and that's why Mam didn't get a kidney.

I was feeling really down and depressed that our life was continuing to be defined by Mam's kidney dialysis. Her twice weekly hospital trips were now going to continue indefinitely unless another new kidney was found and was suitable for Mam.

I felt my future was uncertain, Mam's future was uncertain and nothing I could do would change that.

But something *was* about to change.

Chapter 14

Untruths Unravel

Mam and how she had been reacting and behaving aroused my suspicions so I began to analyse her behaviour.

I wondered why Mam hadn't got the tiniest bit excited or enthusiastic when she knew there was a chance of finally receiving a kidney transplant. A transplant that would dramatically improve her quality of life or even save her life. The impact of a transplant would make a massive difference to our family life. We could be a normal family again, doing the things that normal families do. I knew the operation to transplant a kidney would be serious and not without major risks, but surely Mam would have shown some emotion. I tried to work out why she didn't show the teeniest bit of disappointment when the hours passed by and there was no phone call from the hospital. There was no sign of sadness or dejection with the realisation that the possibility or likelihood of a transplant was diminishing.

I asked myself why it was only Mam and no-one else that heard the phone ring, the call from the hospital, and it was only Mam that had been told about the possible kidney transplant that day. Grandma, Robert and me were all in our house on that cold October morning and neither Robert nor me heard the phone ring and nor did Grandma. Was there really a phone call from the hospital? What time did the hospital phone? Why didn't we hear the phone ring? Why didn't we hear Mam talking on the telephone? Why didn't the hospital phone to say the transplant wasn't going ahead? Surely the hospital would phone. They're caring people and I felt sure they wouldn't want to keep Mam in suspense any longer that was necessary. Why wasn't Mam excited about the transplant? Why wasn't Mam hugely disappointed that it didn't happen? So many questions but no answers.

I then started to think about when our dog Mac bit my leg and when I phoned the Dialysis unit at the hospital to speak to Mam and they told me they didn't have anyone of that name as either an in-patient or out-patient. Why? How could that be so? Was the hospital mistaken or was Mam lying?

I thought about when Alfie had to go into the same hospital where Mam went for her dialysis and I remembered that I had asked her if we could go along to the Ward where she would get her dialysis treatment so I could see what it looked like as she spent so much time there. I remembered Mam's angry response and that she was quite aggressive and very adamant that I couldn't go and take a look because the hospital didn't allow it for safety reasons. I pleaded that I just wanted to look from the corridor, other people were in the corridor, and I wouldn't venture into the Ward, but the clear and firm response was 'NO'. Why?

I thought about the time when I asked Mam about how the hospital gave her the dialysis treatment and she pointed to a scar on her leg. I remembered seeing that scar many years before she started going to the hospital. The scar she showed me was actually a healed wound which she got when she fell over the washing prop many, many years previously. Why would she lie about the scar?

And then, there's Joe. Why does Mam spend so much time looking after him and attending to his every whim and fancy? Why does Joe sometimes take Mam, me and my brothers out for a run in his car, but only when Dad is away?

What about the picture of Mam that I found in Joe's flat? Why was Mam at the pub? Why was she dressed in clothes and jewellery that I'd never seen before? Why did Joe have the picture? Why would Joe want the picture?

It was like lots of pieces of a jigsaw were floating about in my head, but I still couldn't make sense of it all. My head was full of suspicion and confusion. Everything seemed muddled and unclear. I began to question my own thoughts and why I was the only one who seemed to have suspicions. I felt very alone and isolated. There was no-one to turn to, no-one who would listen to me and give me answers to my questions. Grandma, who I was really close to, would just say, in her gentle Scottish accent, 'shish' meaning be quiet. I couldn't ask Dad because if he found out what I knew, was thinking or suspected, he would be absolutely heartbroken. Dad loved his wife despite her many faults.

I felt I was caught up in a living nightmare and in an era when children were seen but not heard. I had no option but to continue to maintain the pretence even though I absolutely did not condone Mam's actions. For the time being, my suspicions and the questions I posed to myself, remained unanswered.

As the days went by and I reflected on the events of previous Thursday I knew the only way to find out the truth (or so I thought) was to talk to Mam. If I talked to her directly I could try to get some answers to my many questions, but I was really afraid to ask her in case I made her angry or upset. Upsetting Mam could create a tsunami of reactions. It could make her shout loudly, it could make her very aggressive, it could make her illness worse. Mam would often take to her bed for hours or days saying she was ill. She would take lots of pills. Pills from the Chemist, pills prescribed by the doctor and many other lotions and potions. She seemed to have an unhealthy obsession with chemicals and formulations.

It never took much to send Mam to her bed. If me or my brothers were the least bit naughty she would start to cry, and tell us that she was going to put us in a children's home because we had made her ill and then she would either take a tablet, several tablets or go for a lie down, or both.

Often it was Robert who was threatened with going to a children's home. Sylvie would pretend to phone the Nuns at the local convent to come and collect him. It was so unimaginably upsetting for me Robert and Alfie. Robert would go to his bedroom, pack a carrier bag and his Beano comic and wait for the Nuns to come. I would sit, crying, with Robert. The Nuns never came.

Mam regularly caused dramas or crises to get attention and we were mostly blamed for causing her to have an 'episode'. We were made to feel responsible for making her more ill and putting her life at risk. This made us feel really bad and often upset me. It created a lot of tension within the house.

Because of my suspicions life at home was becoming very uncomfortable and tensions were heightening. Maintaining what I knew to be a pretence didn't sit comfortably with me and it was starting to affect me quite badly. It was causing me to be anxious and I constantly felt miserable, confused and alone. I was finding it difficult to cope and decided I needed to talk to Mam.

I clearly remember it was a sunny Tuesday with a cool wind blowing from the North and as I walked home from school I decided that today was the day I would talk to Mam.

Mam was in the kitchen preparing Joe's tea as she had done many, many times before. I felt a sudden rage come over me that Joe was being put before our family yet again and that for me was the final straw! I took a deep breath, bit the bullet and blurted out to Mam 'I'm going to tell Dad what's going on with you and Joe'. I suddenly felt a huge sense of relief. For the first time in many years I had actually summoned the strength to stand up and confront Mam. I felt proud of myself!

Mam was clearly enraged and incensed by what I had just said. Within moments she went absolutely crazy, her eyes were full of anger and rage as she turned and picked up a large wooden pick axe handle and started wielding it and swinging it around. She was like a possessed wild woman.

She plunged towards me and started to hit me with it. The first swipe went across my shoulders as I bent forwards to try and avoid its full force. I was absolutely terrified and truly scared for my life. I knew I could be quicker than Mam and that I needed to escape the house before she hit me again and I hurt so much that I would be physically unable to escape.

I didn't know where to escape to. I couldn't think straight. I needed to run away to somewhere safe so I ran straight to my Grandma's house as fast as my legs would carry me to hide under her bed. I fell forwards and laid down on the floor, quickly crawling and scrambling under the bed, pushing a large china chamber pot to one side. I remember being really worried that the chamber pot I had just moved might have wee in it and some of that wee might have splashed on me!

I was well hidden under the bed and I was being as quiet as I could. I thought I was safe. I wasn't! Mam had chased me all the way to Grandma's. I could hear her loud and angry voice as she burst into the house shouting and screaming at the top of her voice 'where is she, where is she hiding'. As she looked around she spotted my left foot quivering and shaking under the bed. She got hold of my feet and dragged me out from under the bed. She continued to hit me with the pick axe handle, her strikes were long, hard and intense. I was screaming in pain and pleading with Mam to stop.

Grandma looked really shocked at what was happening before her eyes. She had no idea what was happening and why Mam was acting in such an aggressive and irrational way. Grandma in her soft Scottish voice started talking to Mam and after a minute or two she managed to calm her down and persuade Mam to return back home.

Shaking, sobbing and hurting from the intense physical abuse, I tried to explain to Grandma what I had said to Mam and why Mam had become so angry. I told her exactly what I had said to Mam. Grandma sat quietly in her wooden armchair and listened to me as I kneeled on the floor beside her. She handed me some toilet tissue to wipe away my tears and put a comforting hand on my shoulder, gently stroking my hair.

Grandma didn't say a word or make any comment. She just said 'whist 'April, which meant be quiet and I was. I think Grandma probably had suspicions about what was going on between Mam and Joe but she didn't want to upset Dad, me or my brothers. The idea of challenging Sylvie was never an option!

I stayed at Grandma's for a few hours, until I felt that it was safe to go home. I was very anxious, even petrified about going home. I didn't know if Mam would still be angry or how she was going to react. I didn't know if I would be safe at home. My arms, shoulders and legs were bruised and sore from what had happened earlier and I didn't want to face more anger and violence. I cautiously opened the front door and went inside. Robert and Alfie were watching TV, Dad was away working and Mam was ...... at Joe's! I felt a huge sense of relief that she wasn't in the house. Mac, our dog was SO happy to see me and jumped up to lick my face. I winced as his heavy paws pressed on my bruised shoulders.

I was hungry so I went into the kitchen and quickly made myself a sandwich before Mam came back. I wolfed it down with a glass of orange pop and then went to my bedroom, curling up on the bed and cuddling my Sindy dolls and reflecting on what a day it had been. I just wanted the day to end but I went to sleep fearful of what the next day would bring.

As I woke up on Wednesday morning, barely able to move without excruciating pain, I felt that yesterday was a real turning point in my relationship with Mam. I didn't think I could ever ask her any questions ever again. I was certainly not going to make any accusations. I think Mam now realised I was growing up and that I could understand what was going on around me and that I had suspicions about her behaviours and actions *and* about her relationship with Joe.

Mam knew that I was becoming more independent, more confident, more self-assured and much less reliant on her and she didn't like it. She really didn't like it!

House fire

Chapter 15

Fear, Fire and Fury

As the years went by very little changed within our family home except we moved from a flat into a terraced house. Dad was working locally as a roofer and by this time Robert had left school and was helping Dad as a trainee roofer. Dad and Robert worked really well together and Robert enjoyed learning new skills from Dad. I was on a YTS scheme and then I got a job as a nanny.

My Mam continued to help Joe and seemed to be spending more and more time at his flat. It was clear from the amount of time she spent there that she must have been doing more than just making meals and cleaning. I'm sure Dad had suspicions or some sort of an inkling as to what was going on but he just seemed to turn a blind eye to it - anything for an easy life.

I met a boy called Martin, my first real boyfriend. After going out together for a short while my Mam was insistent that we moved into a flat together. Dad wasn't at all happy about this and said I couldn't leave home unless I got married. Mam worked her magical manipulative madness and, through her many contacts, got a flat for me and Martin just a few doors away from her. I was working as a Nanny for a local family and Martin was a labourer for a local building firm.

Mam knew she was starting to lose her control over me but she was, after all, still ill and continuing to receive dialysis treatment twice a week and even though I had left the family home Dad, Robert and Alfie were still living there and Joe still had his needs, so I was kept close by to service those needs.

As we were getting older and starting to make our own way in life, making and taking decisions, Mam realised that she was starting to lose her control over all of us. This was another turning point in her behaviours. She became more and more unreasonable and her extreme behaviours escalated to a level not known before.

Our lives were continually impacted by one crisis after another and within my Mam's family there were family feuds, gossiping, fall outs and criminal activity

Around this time there was a tragic accident. Nana Nell was a grandmother to 15 children but she was never what you would call a traditional grandma. In the 1990s Nana Nell's youngest son Geordie and his wife Deb moved into a flat next door to her with their two children. John was the eldest. John was a lovely young boy with white blonde curly hair. He liked school and enjoyed football. He had many of the qualities of Deb his Mam as he could be quiet and solemn. Nana Nell was a big part of their lives and had a lot of control. Geordie and Nana Nell together were quite a force to be reckoned with.

One Saturday nana Nell was going shopping in the city centre and she always expected Deb to go with her.

John, who was 9 years old, did not want to go shopping because he wanted to play football with his friends. Deb and Nana Nell went to town and left John playing football with his friends. If he needed anything he was told to go to Aunty Sylvie's. I was in my early 20's and I was at my Mam's when there was a knock on the door at around mid-day. A local woman came to tell us that people were saying John had been knocked over by a bus and he was lying dead beside the school field.

We were overwhelmed with panic, shock and disbelief.

Mam and I rushed to the school field. As we approached we could see several policemen surrounding the scene and preventing the public and us from getting to John. John had been covered in a blanket. There was a huge pool of blood on the roadside. There was a single ambulance, police cars on the scene. Just along the road was a yellow double decker bus. We were absolutely distraught. There was nothing we could do. I supported and guided Mam back home.

My thoughts quickly turned to Deb and I felt sick to the stomach. John had been playing football on the school field with his friends. The ball went over the fence and he ran on to the road to get it. His friends had shouted that a bus was coming but John seemed oblivious to their words and more concerned about his new ball being burst by a passing car.

Deb was devastated, she was heartbroken. I tried to support her and her younger child but the whole situation was tragic although the news of John's death brought different reactions from different people.

The funeral was a big affair with open back trucks full of flowers which followed the cortege. The funeral brought the attention that some family members craved and there were gangsters and people from the criminal community involved.

The Wake was held in both Nana Nells and Geordie and Deb's houses. The criminal fraternity were in Nana Nell's house and Deb's loving and caring family were in her house.

Almost immediately after the funeral Deb returned to stay with her family in the West End as she couldn't bear to live in the flat without John. Deb was going to a quiet and safe place where she could grieve for John.

The weeks and months that followed were difficult and the impact of the loss of John was huge.

Many months went by and for the first time in quite a while I was looking forward to the summer. The family I was working for as a Nanny were going away for 6 weeks so didn't need me to look after their children. They were happy with the work I did so paid me a retainer to ensure I would still work for them after the summer break. I was really looking forward to having a six week break and enjoying the British summer weather. Sadly, Mam was having none of it. She never liked to see me enjoying myself and seemed to take every opportunity she could to make sure I didn't. A couple of weeks into the holiday Mam attempted suicide. It wasn't the first time and wouldn't be the last. She never took enough tablets that would seriously damage her health or kill her, but just enough to get everyone's attention and sympathy. I spent the next days and weeks checking on her to make sure she was okay.

I was aware that Joe had asked Sylvie to go on holiday to Turkey with him for two weeks. She alluded to the fact that he had just expected her to go. She really wanted to go because it meant that she and Joe could have uninterrupted time together. She needed to work out how she could be with Joe for two whole weeks and probably just expected that we would encourage and support her to go but it was just too bizarre and we just left her to it. We could not have known what lengths she would go to! Sylvie couldn't find a way of being away for two weeks without causing suspicion so she told Joe she couldn't go. Joe told her 'if you can't go then it's over'. Sylvie was desperate to find a way to allow her to go without arousing suspicion. Sylvie loved Joe deeply and didn't want to lose him. Sylvie needed a plan!

Mam was still recovering from her suicide attempt and had lots of time to work out a way in which she could go to Turkey. I called in to check on Mam each day just to make sure she was ok. I still cared even though our relationship was starting to deteriorate.

I had just settled into bed with my book when I got a call on the intercom. It was Mam, saying her house was on fire. Martin and I jumped out of bed, quickly got dressed and ran across to the house. There were no signs of flames but Sylvie was in her dressing gown. I couldn't see any flames or even smell a burning fire. Was Mam imagining things? Was she hallucinating? I decided to open the lounge door only to be met with an intense heat and a fire that was raging. There were ferocious red, yellow and orange flames shooting across the room and along the ceiling. I quickly shut the door and then dragged Mam out of the house.

We stood outside and a neighbour came over to tell us that she had called the fire brigade. They arrived really quickly, cordoned off the area and quickly unreeled their hoses and starting dampening the flames. All I could hear was the noise of wood, crackling and spitting as the water put out the flames. Sparks were flying from the windows and flames escaping out of the doors. The heat coming from the house was unbearable. The smell was unbearable and our lovely home was now a black, smouldering ruin.

Neighbours had gathered outside and stood there, in the dark, with smoke-filled air, staring at the burnt-out mess. They were speechless. It was devastating!

I wondered how Mam knew there was a fire in the house. When Martin and I got to the house minutes after Mam had alerted us there were no obvious signs of a fire so how could Mam know that there was a fire. Shockingly I knew in my heart of hearts that it was my Mam, Sylvie, who had started it.

Although Mam seemed a little shaken she did not show any true signs of shock or distress and seemed almost oblivious to the fact that her home had almost been burned to the ground and absolutely everything had been lost.

I decided the best thing to do was to take Mam over to Nana Nell's, Sylvie's Mam. Mam walked into her house, still wearing her dressing gown. Nana Nell looked straight at Mam, her eyes fixed directly on Mam's eyes.

Her face didn't convey sympathy, care or concern just anger. Standing close to Mam and bending forward Nana Nell said "Sylvie, you've done this". Sylvie didn't flinch, didn't deny what Nana Nell had said. She just turned her head away, walked towards the big armchair and calmly sat down. Even though I thought Mam may have started the fire I was still shocked that Nana Nell had the same thoughts and was strong enough to come right out and say them to Mam.

Mam didn't seem to care that those closest to her were accusing her of starting the fire and was just happy that now she had an unequivocal and cast- iron reason why she wasn't able to go on the two-week holiday with Joe.

After taking Mam to Nana Nell's I went to the Club where Dad was having a quiet drink and told him that the house was on fire and that the Emergency services were doing their best to save the house. Dad couldn't quite believe what he was hearing. He got up from his seat, rushed out of the club and as he ran towards the house all he could see were flames and smoke and the Fire Brigade doing their best to distinguish the flames. Dad was in utter and complete shock. The family home was no more. Only a black shell was left. All that could be seen was black rubble and ash. Sheer devastation!

Every single thing the family had ever owned was gone. Dad was trembling, tears rolling down his cheeks and I tried to comfort him as he tried to comfort me. It was all too much and too devastating to take in. I walked with Dad to Nana Nell's. He looked straight at Sylvie, just as Nana Nell did, and said "you did this". Sylvie didn't utter a word. Her face said it all.

The hours and days that followed the fire were torrid. The whole family, except Sylvie, were consumed with every emotion possible - sadness, devastation, loss, anguish, heartache, anger, but Dad kept positive and always had hope. Much to Sylvie's annoyance, Dad was determined that he would work hard and build back the family home.

Dad, true to his word, worked day and night to clear all of the burnt rubble from the rooms. Nothing could be salvaged. Not a thing. Everything had gone. Furniture, fittings, memorabilia, photographs, the football and sporting trophies we had won. There was absolutely nothing left. Worse still Mam and Dad weren't insured so there was no money to help replace the things that were lost.

Neighbours and friends rallied around to help us where they could. The local press did a feature about the fire in their newspaper which included a picture of Sylvie standing in the burnt remains of the family home.

Dad decided he would stay and sleep overnight at the house while it was being rebuilt to prevent it from deteriorating and to prevent anyone or anything from making things worse, if that was even possible.

Over the next days, weeks and months Dad continued to stay at our burnt-out house spending every spare moment removing blackened furnishings and broken windows before he could start to re-build it. I don't know where Dad got his strength from or what Dad really thought about the fire and the devastation it had caused or how he thought the fire had started. He just remained steadfast in his focus on making things right again and rebuilding the family home as best as he could.

Dad and me didn't talk about the fire either. It was such a painful, worrying and turbulent time I didn't want to mention anything to Dad about my worries or suspicions. It didn't feel right for me to tell him that I, too, thought Mam was an arsonist and that she had started the fire for her own selfish reasons.

Even though I felt an overpowering sense of resentment towards Mam I knew that I still needed to be the dutiful daughter and make sure that she was looked after and cared for. Initially Mam and my brothers moved into my flat whilst Dad continued to work on the family home.

Chapter 16

Hospitals and Holidays

In the dark and traumatic days that followed the fire I struggled to come to terms with the knowledge that it was, without doubt, Mam that started the fire and destroyed everything - all of our possessions and our family life. I was consumed with an overpowering sense of resentment towards her although, stupidly, I still felt the need to be a dutiful daughter and make sure that she, her needs and here welfare were being looked after. She was, after all, my Mam, the person I should be able to trust my life with.

Our family life was in tatters, our family home was gone. Dad, me and my brothers were distraught but Mam, well, Mam just took it all in her stride. In the aftermath of the fire Mam and my brothers moved into my small flat whilst Dad began the long and difficult job of rebuilding the family home.

The weekend following the fire Mam decided to stay at Geordie and Deb's flat as they had moved out temporarily following the death of their son John several weeks earlier. Nana Nell took Mam over to the flat before she went to work as she still held a set of keys and let her into the partly furnished flat.

Dad was absolutely determined that he would rebuild the family home. Mam played no part in helping Dad and stayed well away from the burnt house. On one occasion I was helping Dad to clear the rubble, charred wood and furnishings from the fire damaged house when, for some reason, I thought I should go around and check on Mam to make sure she was ok.

I went around to the flat where Mam was staying and knocked on the door. No answer. I banged on the door several more times, each time harder and louder than the time before but still no answer.

I was becoming anxious and starting to panic and fearing for the worst, I ran over to Grandads house with Martin and we grabbed Grandads window cleaning ladders. We propped them up against the wall, climbed the ladders and looked through the bedroom window. Mam was on the floor, motionless. We were both panic-stricken. All we could do to help her was to break the window and climb in.

We quickly got to her and grabbed her by the shoulders and started shaking her, shouting out her name loudly. Within moments her eyes opened and she started to come around. She told us that she had taken an overdose of tablets.

Another one of many suicide attempts. She never took large overdoses that might do serious damage but just enough to cause concern and attract the attention she always craved.

Fearing for her welfare we rang 999 for an ambulance. We helped her to her feet and, supporting her bodyweight on each of our shoulders, we walked her around the bedroom to make sure she remained conscious until the Ambulance service arrived.

The Ambulance arrived pretty quickly with blue lights flashing and the siren blaring. The Ambulance crew carried out lots of different checks, listening to her heart, taking her blood pressure and temperature.

When the checks were completed they thought it was best if Mam went to the hospital to be thoroughly checked over. Mam agreed to their suggestion and was lifted onto a stretcher. The Paramedics carefully and slowly carried the stretcher down the stairs and into the back of the ambulance. Martin and I felt relieved that we had got to Mam in time and that the hospital would now care of her.

Whilst the Paramedics were making Mam comfortable in the ambulance I ran over the road to get Dad. Dad was still working on the charred remains of the house and his body was covered in burnt black ash. His face was so blackened he resembled a chimney sweep. I told Dad what had happened and he raced over to the back of the ambulance. We both looked on as the ambulance crew were attaching a range of different wires and equipment to different parts of Mam's body.

Dad was desperate and distraught and sooty tears trickled down his cheeks. He told the paramedics that Mam was a dialysis patient. Anyone who receives dialysis treatment must have a specialised form of emergency care so on hearing this the paramedics looked at each other and then started to pull disconnect the wires and drips that they had just inserted.

I knew I had to say something. I went with my gut instinct and blurted out "Dad, she's not having dialysis, you have to believe me". I could see the paramedics glances between each other – understandably they were confused, Dad was confused. But Dad knew that I was telling the truth and believed me, he knew I *always* told the truth. I went into the back of the ambulance with Mam, her eyes just glared at me, she spoke no words to me, to Dad or to the Paramedics. She knew that her game was over!

Dad didn't go in the ambulance with Mam. He stayed behind and went back to clearing the burnt house. I looked at Dad and could see that he was bewildered. He looked as though he was a man who, for the first time, realised that his life with the woman he loved had been one long lie.

Being in the ambulance on the journey to hospital was surreal. The paramedics were quiet and Mam seemed unconscious and, for just a moment, I didn't care. My emotions were numb. I had left Dad, his life completely shattered and it was me who blew the whistle. The realisation that everything, absolutely everything, was one big lie. Our lives had been a lie but I believed the lies because it was my Mam and she is the person you are meant to trust. She had spun a huge and intricate web of lies and I lived within those lies. I was part of the lies and the lies were continuing all because she wanted to go on a holiday to Turkey with Joe.

The hospital was only a few miles away so it wasn't long before the ambulance arrived at the front entrance of the hospital. The paramedics securely strapped Mam to the stretcher and wheeled her out of the ambulance and headed for the Emergency Department.

Nurses guided the paramedics to a cubicle and, with the help of a doctor and nurse Mam was transferred from the stretcher to a bed where a nurse pulled the plain green curtains around all sides of the bed.

Feeling nervous and worried about what would unfold before me I watched on as a series of doctors and nurses wafted in and out of the cubicle. The ambulance crew had passed on information to the doctors about being unsure if Mam was or was not a dialysis patient. I could see from the quizzical expressions on the faces of the doctors that they were concerned and a little confused about how they would proceed with treatment, especially if she was a dialysis patient.

The doctors and nurses spent hours physically examining Mam, checking her blood pressure, taking bloods, assessing the results. They also thoroughly examined all of their hospital records.

Whilst all this was happening I was anxiously waiting in the hospital corridor when my brothers Robert and Alfie arrived. They were really concerned and wanted to know what had happened to Mam. After a little while we went to a room where the nurses were still searching for Mam's medical records. I said to my brothers "please listen to me, I know this sounds really mad but Mam is not a dialysis patient and never has been". My comments didn't seem to come as any surprise to Robert. I think he had been suspicious for some time. Alfie looked shocked.

Only moments later a Doctor came over to me and told me that Mam was not a dialysis patient and was not suffering from kidney failure. He assured us that she was okay.

So, the game was finally up! Mam had lied for years and years to her children. She had lied to her husband. She had lied to family and friends. Mam had spent years coercing everyone into believing that she was ill and that she might die. She had consistently lied about having dialysis treatment, first having treatment once a week and then having treatment twice a week and then waiting for a kidney transplant. She had lied about the scar on her leg and not being able to drink alcohol because it would affect her treatment and all the time she was having an affair with our neighbour Joe and spending 'dialysis' evenings enjoying herself and drinking alcohol in a pub.

I felt totally betrayed. Mam had betrayed us all. Our childhoods and our family life had been a litany of lies. Our childhoods had been lost!

We were all shocked. It was a lot for us to take in. I knew I had my really strong suspicions about Mam but I always tried to find a reason to counteract what I thought were lies. I always wanted to see the best in Mam and I wanted to trust her. I never confided in Dad, I never told him about my suspicions, because they were just that, suspicions and I didn't want to hurt him. Maybe, on reflection, I was just a child and I should have talked to him but I knew that Mam would manipulate everything and this would probably damage our already fractured relationship with Dad.

The nurses came and talked to me and my brothers and offered more reassurance that Mam was okay but that she would be staying in hospital overnight. The nurse told us that we were allowed to see her before we went home. Robert and Alfie decided not to see Mam, they were feeling angry and betrayed. I went into the cubicle alone and pulled back the curtains. I had such mixed emotions and I was struggling with what to say. After a moment I just blurted out "I could kill you"! She just looked at me emotionless. Her response was "go home April, get some rest, you've had a long day". Unbelievable!

She then told me to ring Joe to tell him that she was okay but would be staying overnight in hospital and that he could come and visit her! Unbelievable! Her request infuriated me and made me feel sick to the stomach with despair. Mam showed no remorse, she had no regrets and no sense of shame about her lies, about what had just been exposed or what she was telling me to do. I didn't phone Joe. There was no way that I was ever going to phone Joe. Joe was just as much a part of this as Sylvie.

I don't know if Joe did visit Mam, but I didn't care. I despised Joe for what he did to our family. Early the next day Mam left hospital, bright and breezy with a smile on her face as though nothing out of the ordinary had happened.

Dad and the builders were making good progress on rebuilding the house and it was getting ever-closer to the point where it could be decorated internally and furnished. Dad had worked so hard and he had done an amazing job. Mam played no part in helping to rebuild the family home. In fact, she spent much of the time in bed. Dad continued to look after Mam, attending to her every whim and fancy because she was still 'vulnerable and fragile'.

Mam's perceived fragility and vulnerability seemed to prevent Dad from confronting her about her lies. He didn't ask her about the house fire or about the dialysis. Mam was still managing to manipulate everyone for her own selfish needs.

I could hardly believe it but secretive rendezvous were still going on with Joe as the time for the Turkey holiday trip was fast approaching. Mam needed to hatch a plan and hatch a plan she did! Mam was good at hatching plans, she'd been doing it for years! Mam told us all, in no uncertain terms, that her health had severely suffered because of all the recent traumas and that she needed a break away from it all to recover.

She told us that she was going to Turkey for two weeks with her cousin Melissa. It sounded plausible enough but Sylvie's cousin Melissa was another figment of her imagination and was created to serve as a smokescreen for her true intentions.

As the day of departure drew closer Sylvie must have felt a mix of exhilaration and guilt. She knew she was deceiving her family but she also knew that this time away with Joe was an opportunity they both desperately wanted and needed. They seemingly yearned for two weeks of uninterrupted time together where they could explore their love and forge deeper connections.

The day of the holiday arrive and with her bags packed and her heart pounding Sylvie bid her farewell to us all, promising to send postcards and to phone regularly. So, off she went to the airport for a two-week holiday, to stay in a hotel - in the sun, with *Joe* aka Melissa!

Chapter 17

Home Again

With Mam away in Turkey for two whole weeks me, dad and my brothers set about putting the final touches to what had been a completely burnt-out shell to make it into our cosy family home once again.

Dad had worked relentlessly, mainly on his own but with limited help from the builders. It was now time for me and my brothers to pull together and help Dad get the house finished. Working with my Dad brought us all closer together, closer than we had been for years because there was no interference from Mam. We worked hard painting and decorating the rooms, putting in new fixtures, fittings and furnishings. The decor and the house were looking absolutely fantastic. The house was clean bright and fresh – such an amazing achievement in a short space of time.

Although Dad had thrown every bit of his heart and soul into rebuilding the house I think he also used the time as a distraction to ignore or deflect his feelings of pain and hurt that were all caused by Mam. I don't think he wanted to admit that his world had been torn apart and that he was hurting. but I could see the pain and the hurt in his eyes, I could see the emotional and psychological pain that Mam had inflicted. I knew, despite everything, that Dad still loved her and still wanted to be with her. I really didn't like how Mam had lied and lied not only to me, my brothers and Dad but to our wider family.

Mam was never far from my thoughts even though she was out of the country. I remembered that she had left a letter for me before she flew off to Turkey. I picked up the letter and carefully opened it wondering what words or message would be contained within it and whether those words would be the truth or lies. She had chosen the words within the letter very carefully. She wrote that she loved me and she loved my brothers. She said she would not be enjoying her time in Turkey and that she only went under the duress of Joe. She wrote that everything would be better and different when she returned home because she couldn't live without us.

I so wanted the words in that letter to be true but how could I trust her, she had lied so many times and for so many years. How could I believe her now? How could she change? Why would she want to change?

I spent some time imagining how Sylvie and Joe would have been spending their time in Turkey. Maybe they would be exploring breath-taking landscapes, indulging in romantic dinners, sharing laughter and tears, revelling in the joy of being together, cherishing every moment as though it were their last. Maybe they were just reading and relaxing on sunbeds. One thing I did know was that when they returned to England they would face the consequences of their actions and their deception.

Even though Mam would have many questions to answer when she returned home I was feeling more and more resentful about my lost childhood. I was always there for Mam but she was never really there for me. The enormity of her lies, her manipulation and control influenced me when I was growing up and as an adult. I started to think about all of the things I missed out on, the different occasions and events that had been ruined or negatively impacted because of Mam.

I thought about how my Dad always provided love and stability and was a constant presence in my life and my brothers. It was Dad who taught us to tell the time, how to tie our shoelaces, he took us to the beach and the park. Dad made our Go-Carts and bought us bikes.

Even though Dad often worked away, his children were always his priority and always in his thoughts. If he had been abroad he might have been away for 10 or 12 weeks and on return Dad would open his huge mustard-coloured suitcase to reveal presents, thoughtful presents that he had chosen for us all.

Dad, just like Grandad Alf, had lots of patience and lots of time for me and my brothers. When he had been working abroad his thick dark hair would often change colour because of the sun so there would be a tinge of redness at the roots. When he was working in the hot sun his back would get burned and me, Robert and Alfie loved to slowly peel off the dead skin.

Dad loved all fresh seafood and whenever he was at home there was always lots of it in the kitchen. He would buy fresh crabs, mussels and prawns and prepare them all for us to eat. Mam was never keen on fish as she didn't like the smell and would leave us to enjoy it whilst she stayed in the kitchen. She would always fling open the windows to get rid of any fishy smells.

I think Mam was jealous of the relationship we had with Dad and did her best to create an atmosphere where we might fear Dad. She tried destroying our relationship with him by convincing us that he was unreasonable and that she was a victim of his behaviour. Over the years we listened and trusted what Mam told us about Dad and we gave her the attention she craved because we believed and loved her.

Mam was very different to Dad in so many ways. I often wondered why Mam was so popular with neighbours and friends. Then I realised that she possessed a unique charm and charisma that seemed to effortlessly attract friends. It was as if she had a magnetic personality that drew people towards her but in reality. She was manipulating them like she manipulated me. She really was an expert, a master in the manipulation of anything and anyone. She could groom people and go to great lengths to achieve her aims, to achieve what *she* wanted.

When we were young she would make us shoplift when we were out shopping with her. When she worked in a local shop she stole stock and money, she set up a fake robbery with her brother so it appeared she had been ambushed and the takings from the shop had been stolen. These are not the actions of a loving Mother.

I remember the day after the 'robbery', Paul, the local copper came to the house to see her. I remembered seeing Paul when I was younger and when we went to the Fish Van to get fish every Friday. He would often be sat in his car and we would climb into the back of it whilst Mam talked to the copper. From what I overheard she was giving him information about criminal activity that was going on in and around the neighbourhood. She even gave information about her own family's criminal activity to detract from what she had done. There were no bounds to what Mam would do to protect herself or achieve what she wanted to achieve.

Whilst Mam was in Turkey Dad had time to reflect and think about various events and happenings over the past months and years. He started to connect the events and to put two and two together. He knew Joe worked at British Rail so decided to phone his office and ask to speak to him. He was told that Joe was on two weeks holiday. In Dad's mind that confirmed that Sylvie was on holiday with Joe. Dad decided that he would go to the airport and meet Sylvie and Joe in the Arrivals Lounge.

Sylvie knew nothing of her husband's suspicions but as the day approached for her and Joe to return, her heart grew heavy with the weight of her secret. She knew that honesty would be the only way to move forward, to rebuild the trusts she had shattered. She braced herself for the storm that she thought would await her when she arrived home. Little did she know that her deceit had already been uncovered.

Emotions were high as Robert and Dad made their way to the bustling Airport together. The air was thick with tension and their footsteps echoed the anxiety that filled their hearts. They were on their way to conform Sylvie and Joe.

Dad and Robert stood together, shoulder to shoulder, feet firmly anchored to the ground. Their minds were racing with a multitude of questions, frustration, hurt and betrayal. Frank couldn't make sense of why Sylvie would do this to their already fragile family.

The plane from Turkey had landed and Dad and Robert were scanning the crowd, searching for Mam and Joe when, finally, they spotted them, hand-in-hand, Sylvie's eyes sparkling like a woman in love.

Sylvie spotted her family and the look on her face changed, her eyes widened with a mixture of shock and guilt. "I didn't expect you to be here" she said, with her voice trembling. Dad's gaze hardened, his jaw clenched as he tried to contain his emotions. "You didn't expect us to be here? You left to go away with your cousin Melissa, a cousin that doesn't exist and now you return hand-in-hand, laughing and joking with Joe, how could you!"

Robert asked "why did you leave us Mam, why did you go away with Joe, why did you lie?"

Mam's face crumpled with apparent regret, her voice quiet, barely above a whisper and said "I needed to get away, to recover from the pain of the past few weeks. I'm not well".

Dad's voice softened a little and told her that the family was falling apart and we all needed to work together to fix it, not to run away from it.

As they stood in the airport, amidst the chaos they knew that this confrontation was just the beginning of a long and challenging journey towards rebuilding trust and finding forgiveness.

Together, Sylvie, Dad and Robert left the airport to return home and face the rest of the family.

When they arrived at Chester Close it was exceptionally tense, strained, an unreal, even surreal moment. The atmosphere felt tense, the situation bizarre. On the journey home Sylvie had time to think and now she was trying hard to hide the smirk on her face, her satisfaction that the plan she had hatched had worked, she didn't seem bothered or embarrassed that she had been caught-out. In reality she seemed quite confident and comfortable at her deceit and manipulation of everyone.

Although Dad was absolutely devastated, and despite everything that had gone on, he still loved Sylvie and she had promised him that she loved him and wouldn't leave his side again.

Sylvie made out to everyone that *she* was the victim, she told us that she had *never* wanted to go to Turkey but Joe had blackmailed her and told her that she had to go to care for him.

Sylvie told Dad that she loved him and wanted to be with him and not Joe. Dad's love for Mam was so great and so strong that he was sure there was at least a glimmer of hope that they could repair mend whatever it was that was broken. Mam and Dad made the decision together that they would stay together and give things another go.

The reconciliation was short. Very short! Sylvie stayed with Dad in the house for two weeks and then left to live with Joe.

Newcastle Airport

Chapter 18

Claiming and Blaming

Joe moved house and was now living in a house a couple of miles away. My relationship with Mam was difficult and had seriously deteriorated. But, she was still my Mam and I felt a need to maintain some level of contact.

On one of my visits, quite late in the day, I knocked on Mam's door and when she came to open it she was still wearing her nightclothes. Mam told me that Joe was at work and that she had been visited by a Psychiatrist. She told me that the Psychiatrist wanted to see me too. I couldn't work out why a Psychiatrist would want to see me, it seemed rather strange but I was happy to do anything that was needed if it helped our family situation to improve. Mam said she would arrange the appointment at St Nicholas Hospital.

When details of the appointment arrived through the post I felt a little anxious. On the day of the hospital appointment I felt very nervous so I asked my friend Jossie to come with me. I was expecting that the appointment would provide some sort of explanation about why Mam had been behaving in such a destructive way for over 20 years. How wrong could I have been!

The Psychiatrist, a lovely middle-aged lady with greying hair, gently told me that my Mam was blaming me for all the problems that she had. I was completely taken aback. I couldn't believe what I was hearing. Initially I felt angry, confused, annoyed and in disbelief but I gathered my thoughts together and gradually detailed how Mam had been behaving over the years. When I finished I said "Well, please tell me, am I mad, am I the one causing all of the problems?" The Psychiatrist leaned forward in her chair and replied "No, but, if you don't get some help with this soon you will be".

In utter disbelief Jossie and I slowly walked out of the hospital and made our way to the bus stop for the short journey back home.

I tried to rationalise and process what had just happened. Why Mam had accused me of making her ill. I came to the conclusion that this was just another attempt by Mam to show that she was the victim and that she needed and deserved help and support. She truly only cared about herself, her own needs and nobody else. I struggled to come to terms with Mam's persona. How could she not want the very best for her children. I found it very difficult to believe that she was physically ill but it was quite possible that she was psychotic. With all that I knew how could I possibly ever believe anything she said?

A couple of weeks passed by and Mam unexpectedly started to visit the family home. At this point I was still living in a flat with Martin. Dad, Robert and Alfie were living in the lovely refurbished family home. It felt a really positive time and I was hopeful that when Mam began visiting the house she would realise that she wanted to be with her family and had made a terrible mistake by moving in with Joe. But, as usual, she was controlling and manipulating the situation yet again. She was playing with our good nature and emotions.

It was becoming crystal clear that Mam really liked the fully refurbished house with all its new decor, kitchen, appliances and furniture. The house was so much nicer than Joe's house. Mam hatched her plan! She embarked on a course of manipulation and mind-games, something for which she had a natural, or maybe unnatural, talent for. She deflected any blame away from herself and started to turn my brothers against Dad. With simmering anger, she blamed and pointed the finger at Dad for family problems in the past, for making her ill, for not giving her enough money so that she had to steal, for being difficult to live with and for being the reason she moved in with Joe.

The tensions in our house were hostile and suffocating. Dad couldn't take the explosive exchanges anymore. He realised that the family had reached a crossroads. Dad said "look, if you want your Mam to be here instead of me then I'll move out". Despite the web of lies and deceit spun by Mam, despite her illicit affair, it was decided that Mam should move in and Dad should move out. And that's exactly what happened. This is one of *my* biggest regrets.

The only way Dad could afford to move out and buy a property for himself was to sell the house. The house was put up for sale but Mam was seething, she was furious. She knew she couldn't afford to buy it so she talked and talked to Robert until she wore him down and persuaded him to get a mortgage to buy Dad out.

Dad was left with just £10,000, not much after he rebuilt and refurbished the whole house. Dad moved into a flat not very far from my flat. The flat needed to be fully redecorated so whilst Dad was working away we redecorated it for him.

Robert and Alfie were still working with Dad as roofers but their relationships were becoming very strained. Robert seemed to hold a strong grudge against Dad because it was Robert who took out the mortgage on the house to be able to buy out Dad's share. Sylvie was living in the family home but she was still seeing Joe regularly and this caused further tensions with Robert, Alfie and me.

The events of the past few months were starting to take their toll on me and my health was deteriorating. I started to feel emotionally and physically sick. I was experiencing severe anxiety and my relationship with Martin was becoming unhealthy so I decided to end it.

For quite some time, I found it almost impossible to leave home. I think Mam liked the fact that I wasn't able to leave home because she knew where I was. I became, effectively, a prisoner in my own home. There were times when I had dark thoughts and thought I was dying. The advice I was given at the time didn't help and nor did the prescribed medications.

After many months I was referred to the local mental health services but the waiting lists were long. I felt resentful that I was ill and I was exhausted and it was all brought on by the many traumas of childhood and adulthood yet Mam was out and about, thriving and working in clubs with Robert who was now making a name for himself as a DJ.

My ill health continued for quite some time but eventually I gained strength and confidence so that I was able to go out and to go to work. By this time, it's the late 1990's and my Grandad Alf had become ill, so ill that he was admitted to hospital. My Uncle Claude who was also not in good health, was living with Grandma and Grandad at the time. I would often go with Dad to visit Grandad in hospital and when Grandma was well enough we would take her in her wheelchair so she could visit too.

For reasons I can't explain Mam managed to involve herself in visiting Grandad in hospital. She'd never taken much interest in Grandma and Grandads. welfare until now. She would contact Dad and make arrangements to go and visit at the same time that he would visit. After a few joint visits she suggested that they go to the club together after the hospital visit. I couldn't believe she was trying to control and manipulate things again. I didn't want Dad getting hurt again. Mam was still seeing Joe but now she wanted to see Dad. Why?

Whilst Grandad was in hospital I helped to care for Grandma who was now in her 80's and partially sighted. Her daily care needs were increasing to a level that she needed professional care. It was arranged that Grandma went into a respite care facility. I stayed with her until late into the night to help her settle in. Not long after I left her she had a massive stroke. She was transferred to the same hospital as Grandad and was put into a bay right next to him.

Sadly, Grandma died as a result of her stroke and it was only a week later that Grandad died. My sense of loss was massive, I was distraught at losing Grandma and Grandad so close together. Losing them meant the loss of a huge part of my family, the part of my family that had always been good, decent, authentic and who had provided me and my brothers with genuine love and care. I felt very burdened by guilt as the time I could have spent with them was limited and I could have had so much more time with them had it not been for the needs, lies and madness of Mam.

Dad's parents had always played such a big part in my life and in the lives of my brothers. Grandma would play board games with us like Battling Gladiators - her character would always be Terrible Titus so we would often fondly refer to her as Titus. On the 'Dialysis' nights that she baby-sat us we would sit together and watch old musicals with her and Dracula films. Being with Grandma was like being in a safe and loving sanctuary.

It was a desperately sad time with two funerals taking place in quick succession. Grandma and Grandad didn't have many material possessions or much money but what they did have was shared out between Dad, Claude and, of course, Sylvie. All was becoming clear just why Sylvie started to visit Grandad in hospital. Money was Sylvie's great motivator.

Uncle Claude continued to live in Grandma and Grandad's flat. He had a very different character and personality to Dad. Dad was always very practical and organised whereas Uncle Claude was much more of a free spirit. He had a very dry sense of humour and everybody loved him even though he didn't lead the healthiest of lifestyles.

Chapter 19

Struggle to Strength

It was in 1991 that I started to struggle with my health and it took a turn for the worse and was on a downward spiral. I had been suffering back pain for almost eighteen months but the pain was getting worse and worse, particularly at night and I could never find a resting place. I was starting to feel exhausted and my blood pressure was alarmingly high. I was sent for a scan which showed that I had kidney disease. How ironic! Mam had faked kidney disease for years and years and now I had actually been officially diagnosed with kidney disease!

I couldn't speak to Sylvie about it. How could I?

It was around this time that I realised that I was now calling my Mam Sylvie and not Mam. I don't know why I did this but I think, somehow, I wanted to erase the name of Mam from my memory as she was the person who had almost destroyed me and my family.

I was told by the hospital that I needed surgery, major surgery to either remove a kidney or partially remove a kidney. It turned out that doctors were able to partially dissect the diseased kidney and were hoping that what remained would be able to repair itself.

Sylvie came to see me in hospital but somehow managed to flirt and charm my other visitors and visitors of other patients and paid little attention to me. My Dad and Uncle Claude came too and I really appreciated their visits.

My recovery was long and painful and I was told that I would be on medication for the rest of my life. Whilst recovering from the pain of the operation I continued with my battle against anxiety. I had been on the mental health referral list for some time but eventually an appointment came through and I started treatment. I saw a psychiatrist to talk through the many events that had happened throughout my life and how they had impacted on me and on my overall health.

I was scared to talk to professionals. I didn't know where to begin. My life had been shaped by events that are hard for me to believe let alone anyone else. Would they believe me? Would they think I was mad? I was at a critical point and I was exhausted although I didn't realise it at the time.

I worked with a clinical psychologist for over 3 years, together setting goals to help get my life back on track. The goals were things like ending my unhealthy relationship with Martin, getting a job or studying and learning to drive.

After a long time and much willpower, I managed to get my anxiety under control and my overall health started to improve. I was determined to focus and achieve the goals that I had set.

I started working as a Nanny and I was exceptionally fortunate to meet two people who were neighbours of the family I was Nanny to. Their names were Jossie and Chrissie. I feel forever grateful and blessed to have met them because they were absolutely integral and instrumental in supporting me through the issues caused by the madness of my psychotic Mother. Jossie and Chrissie were truly good and nice people from whom I learned so much. They helped gently guide me to change the course of my life.

Jossie and Chrissie both had a background in mental health and wellbeing. There were many days when I just did not want to have therapy sessions but, together they inspired me to keep going. I will forever be grateful for these two good people who came into my life.

As part of my recovery one of my goals was to end my unhealthy relationship with Martin, I had been with him for 13 years. It was a relationship in which Mam had played a major part by bringing us together, finding a flat for us and always being deeply involved in our lives. Because I was only 17 when I began living with Martin I felt resentful that I had missed out on so many of life's opportunities. I ended the relationship.

I enrolled in college and qualified as a Nursery Nurse. Sylvie didn't want me to study and chose every opportunity to discourage me, telling me I wasn't clever enough and it wouldn't pay me enough money. But I ignored Sylvie's advice and I worked part-time whilst I studied. I became involved with a charity providing support services to women and children who were affected by homelessness.

I started to take driving lessons which I found both terrifying and enjoyable in equal measure. I took 3 driving tests. I failed 3 driving tests. I gave up! Maybe this goal was one too many!

In 1996 things were starting to look much brighter for me. I qualified as a Nursery Nurse and was working almost full-time at a Homeless Hostel. I loved the job and have immensely fond memories of working with many children and young people. I found myself identifying with some of the stories they would tell me about the abuse they had suffered or witnessed and I realised that I too had been abused but that I had normalised it.

It was also in 1996 that I began a relationship with Drew, a really good friend I had known for many years. Drew and I got on really well and I felt very relaxed in his company. We decided to get engaged and Drew moved into my flat. Drew and me becoming a couple is one of the best things that has happened in my life.

Unlike Martin, Drew is a strong, kind, caring, honest and trustworthy person. Drew was always strong enough to stand up to Sylvie's narcissistic and controlling ways. Sylvie was never happy when Drew would defend and protect me. After all, she was used to controlling my life from a very young age. Drew has been one of the most positive happenings in my life and has made me feel happy, safe and loved.

Drew and I enjoyed living in our flat, but we were keen to buy our own home. A couple of years after living together we noticed that there was a house for sale within our cul-de-sac and only two doors away from Sylvie. Drew and I were interested in the house and set about finding out how much it was. We worked out our finances and although it would be tight we knew we could afford to buy the house. It was very run-down and needed a lot of work but neither of us was afraid of hard work and we knew that together we could make it into a beautiful home, so we bought the house.

Just as everything seemed to be going well for us I began to feel ill again. I had lots of back pain, like years ago, but this time I had infections too. My GP referred me back to the hospital. I had an appointment within days. I saw the Consultant and he delivered the news I really didn't want to hear. "April I'm sorry to tell you that your kidney did not heal itself after the last operation so we now need to carry out more surgery to fully remove the diseased kidney. This wasn't the news I wanted but I was in so much pain and discomfort I felt a slight sense of relief that the impending surgery would resolve the problems I was having.

The surgery took place only a few weeks after my appointment and it went well. I knew from past experience that the recovery was going to be long and painful, something I wasn't looking forward to. Once again, I felt the unfairness of my real illness and how seriously it was affecting my life and it caused me to reignite my resentment towards Sylvie who had been faking illness for 19 years.

Drew was amazingly supportive and looked after me really well. I never felt very hungry but he would always make me whatever I fancied and would coax me into eating fruit and vegetables.

I had a lot of time to think during my recovery and - at times the thoughts were dark and heavy. I remember the family discussing that I might need a kidney transplant in the future and they were considering the possible donor candidates. Sylvie was never ever mentioned as a possible donor as she had her own kidney problems!! Such was the power of her manipulation, her deceit and lies that she had somehow managed to totally convince the extended family that she really was suffering from kidney failure.

As I was on the road to recovery following my surgery the purchase of our new house was completed and we were given the keys to the door. We were SO happy. I knew, because of the surgery, I was limited to what I could do but I was able to be Drew's labourer. He knocked walls down, he built new walls and I would sweep and clear the debris. As my health improved I was able to return to work. Each night, after work we would go to the house and do more remedial work. Drew worked so hard to make the house our dream home. His skills and work ethic reminded me of Dad rebuilding our house after the fire.

Whilst we were working on the house the relationships with Sylvie's immediate and extended family were deteriorating. There were lots of arguing, family fighting and secrecy going on. This was nothing new, they were always falling out and calling each other. Nana Nell was often at the centre of her son Geordie's criminal activities. She was like a 70 years old gangster granny. She loved the criminal lifestyle, she loved being around petty criminals and gangsters and Mam did too.

Chapter 20

New Beginnings

Sylvie had now moved Joe into what was our family home. The plan she'd hatched to get Dad out of the house and to move Joe in had worked! Joe had sold the house he owned to one of his children for a much-reduced value but he still had lots of money in his pocket.

Sylvie and Joe were now, officially, a couple.

Robert was moving on with his life and had met someone. They soon had a child they called Connor. Mam was furious about his relationship and hated Robert's partner with a vengeance. Their personalities clashed and there was constant drama between them.

Mam's controlling and manipulative behaviour made Robert's life hell. I could recognise the similarities as to how she had been with Dad.

Robert was paying the mortgage on the family home and did not want to continue to have the expense or the responsibility as he was now in a relationship and wanted to buy his own place. Mam was having none of it. She was furious at what he was intending to do and started smashing the contents of the kitchen, something I had seen her do many times before.

Somehow, even though Mam wasn't working, she managed to arrange to take over the mortgage. Nana Nell probably had something to do with it! Within a few weeks Robert left the family home to set up his own home with his new family. For whatever reason Robert's relationship with his partner didn't last for very long. Perhaps it was because his partner had many of the same traits that Mam had. She left their family home and took Connor with her.

At this time Alfie was still living with Mam. He was earning good money as a roofer, the trade that Dad had taught him. He was well liked, quite handsome and enjoyed keeping fit. Alfie had no real responsibilities as Mam did everything for him. He was treated like a prince and she had, quite cleverly, created a dependence on her that meant Alfie would find it difficult to survive on his own and without her support and guidance.

After a while, Alfie met a girl called Sammi and they struck up a lovely friendship which turned into a relationship. They made a very striking couple and had a wide circle of friends. They enjoyed socialising in pubs and clubs and just spending lots of time together doing lovely things together.

For reasons unknown, Alfie started to drink heavily, taking drugs and being involved with a range of risky behaviours which caused him to go 'off the rails'. It was around this time that Sammi found out that she was pregnant.

Sammi talked to Alfie and told him that she was pregnant. She knew that Alfie wouldn't take the news at all well. Alfie was not a person who could deal with responsibility, Mam had seen to that. Alfie's response was that he did not want the responsibility of a baby so, rather than be there for Sammi and support her through her pregnancy, he simply ran off and abandoned her.

We all thought that Alfie would take stock and embrace having a child once he had got over the shock. We thought he would relish the chance of having a new family and a new way of life but, it wasn't to be. He completely refused to have any involvement with Sammi or their baby.

Alfie didn't have any further contact with Sammi and he continued to be controlled by Mam. His lifestyle worsened and he fell into a downward spiral.

Sammi's pregnancy went well and in 1998 she gave birth to a beautiful girl. Sammi named her baby Jade. Sammi was more than happy for me and Drew to be part of her life and we were so happy that we were able to be there for her right from the day she was born.

Jade used to come to stay at Sylvie's every other weekend and Drew and I shared some of that time with her. We so enjoyed our time together. As she got a little older she would pack a little overnight bag and bring it with her to our house when she was sleeping over. Her bag was full of everything she needed for the weekend.

Drew introduced her to horse riding and she learnt to ride a horse and absolutely loved it. We did all sorts of outdoor activities and it was so special to see her confidence and personality grow and develop. We have always been part of her life and she has completely enriched our lives. Watching her grow from a little girl into a beautiful, confident and successful woman has been and continues to be a delight.

To this day we still meet up regularly with Jade for a coffee and chat. Unfortunately, Alfie, her Dad, has never made any effort to meet with her or Sammi.

Although Sylvie has kept regular contact with Sammi and Jade she has never encouraged Alfie to be part of Jade's life. Sylvie's priority was always to control and protect Alfie which included stopping him from taking responsibility.

Alfie was heavily dependent on Sylvie and relied on her support which he struggled with and came to resent. When Drew and I left our rented flat Alfie applied and succeeded in taking on the tenancy. It gave him some space from Sylvie but not nearly enough.

When we were young me and my brothers got on really well and I would always do what I could to protect and care for them. As we became adults Sylvie was such a forceful presence in their lives that our closeness drifted.

Chapter 21

Millennium Mayhem

In September 2000 Drew and me were at our new house, still spending lots of time refurbishing it when, around 7.30 we decided to tidy things up and go back to the flat. The nights were drawing in and it was warm so the windows were open to let the air circulate. I was in the bedroom getting changed when I heard a huge bang and then another bang. The echoing sounds shattered the tranquillity of the Square. They were sounds that I had never ever heard before and I was startled by them.

I heard Drew run over to the window "they've shot Geordie, April, they've shot Geordie". Geordie's van was parked in the Square and you could barely make out the dark shape of a shadowy figure running at speed from the Square. Drew quickly ran down the stairs to see, first hand, what had happened and if he could help. I just froze. My legs turned to jelly.

I managed, somehow, to get down the stairs and into the entrance way. There, right next to Nana Nell's front door was Deb kneeling on the floor with Geordie lying on top of her. The sight of Deb and Geordie was like a scene from a horror movie. There was lots of blood, pools of blood and splattered blood everywhere. In a panic I just ran past them, looking for Drew. Deb was shouting to me "April, April the bairns, get my bairns". I ran to Sylvie's and Sylvie came out like a crazy woman and then chaos erupted, absolute chaos.

In the midst of this sudden eruption of violence a man, Geordie, lay lifeless in a doorway, being supported by Deb who was covered in blood. There was blood seeping from Geordies body and as it flowed from his body it stained the pavement beneath him. The shock of the scene brought the Square to a standstill. Neighbours stood frozen to the ground, their faces a mixture of horror, sorrow and disbelief.

Drew raced back to the square after trying to catch a glimpse of who had carried out this horrific shooting.

The Emergency services were called but would not attend immediately because there was a firearm involved. Drew and I went and got Geordie's and Deb's children who were aged seven and nine as, understandably, they were terrified. We were terrified.

Deb was still holding Geordie, blood was still continuing to trickle from the door entrance right along the path. It was like a scene right out of a movie except, it wasn't a movie, this was real!

After what seemed like an eternity we heard the wailing sirens of the emergency services. Police arrived first and then the ambulance. The Police descended in numbers, their presence commanding authority as they swiftly cordoned off the area, ensuring the safety of the bystanders and preserving the integrity of the crime scene. Some police officers were armed and everyone was firmly told to stand back or to go back into their homes.

The Paramedics rushed to Geordie's side, their faces etched with determination but they were met with the grim reality that their efforts would be in vain. Geordie was given the best treatment available and lifted onto a stretcher and taken to hospital. He succumbed to his injuries and died in the ambulance from gunshot wounds to his head.

The police officers diligently began their investigation and interviewed the shaken witnesses, searching for any clues that could she a light on this senseless act of violence.

Neighbours huddled together, their eyes filled with fear and their voices trembling as they each recounted what they had seen or heard.

One elderly lady, a retired school teacher who lived across the Square, recounted that she was in her kitchen holding a mug of coffee in her frail hands when she heard the gunshot. She said it was so loud it made her drop her mug. She peeked through her curtains and saw Geordie lying there, bleeding so she immediately called the Police.

As the night wore on the police continued with their investigations, searching for any evidence that could bring justice to the man who had lost his life so violently.

The news that Geordie had died spread around the estate quickly. It seemed like everyone had gathered together in Sylvie's house whilst outside there was still mayhem, chaos and a serious crime scene. Police cars, vans and police officers were everywhere. A police helicopter circled above with blue lights flashing on and off and a bright white beam was sweeping from side to side searching the area for the gunman.

We were all in shock but we were doing as Deb asked and looking after Geordies and her two children in the lounge of Sylvie's house. We were trying to protect and shield them from the horror that was unfolding in the Square. Deb was taken to hospital too. It was a miracle that she was not hurt. Deb asked us to tell the children what had happened. It was a difficult and desperate time and we could barely comprehend what had just happened, so how could children possibly understand.

We didn't know the circumstances that led to Geordie being shot or who would want to shoot Geordie. All we knew was that Geordie was dead and a gunman was on the run.

With trepidation we talked to the children. We were as calm, gentle and as compassionate as we could be. We told them that their Dad had tragically died and he would be going to heaven. Both children were distraught, sobbing and completely inconsolable.

The whole Square remained cordoned off with blue and white tape and Police kept a presence for days. It's hard to describe the minutes, hours and days that followed. Me and Drew were in a daze, not able to comprehend what had gone on. Scared that the gunman could come back.

We tried but we couldn't make any sense of why someone would want to hurt, let alone murder Geordie but we were very much alone in our sense of shock and disbelief. Others seemed to have some knowledge or insight as to why the killing took place.

Sylvie and her family were enjoying the limelight caused by Geordie's death. They seemed to be relishing in their gangster status and were more than happy to talk to TV reporters and to the local and national papers about the execution that happened right on their doorstep.

There seemed to be a hive of weird activity going on in the Square with phone calls being exchanged between petty criminals. Perhaps some were thinking that they may be next on the hit list.

Locals were taken into police custody for questioning. Although Drew and I had a very real sense of fear and worry that the perpetrator may return to the Square others showed no concern at all, even though Deb was grieving for her husband and the children were distraught at the loss of their father.

In the weeks that followed the murder Sylvie and Nana Nell were still enjoying their new found 'celebrity' status with the media and their 'gangster' status with the local criminals. They enjoyed the sympathy they received from neighbours but showed no support, thought or consideration towards the immediate grieving family.

Many months later we found out that the shooting of Geordie was part of a high-profile gangland drugs case which involved high profile and dangerous criminals.

Somehow Sylvie and Nana Nell, who were both creative, smart and resourceful, managed to convince friends and neighbours that they were the victims of this horrific shooting. So compelling was their story that they received sympathy from neighbours and friends. In reality the victims were Deb, Geordies wife and her two children.

As the police investigations continued it was discovered that the gunman had hidden in wait within the bushes at our new house when we were actually inside renovating it. Police advised us that it was highly likely that Drew and I passed by the gunman when we left the house to go across the Square and back into our flat.

Some months later the gunman was identified and prosecuted. The high-profile case took place in the High Court in Leeds. The Court was protected by armed police officers and the gunman was convicted and sentenced.

Though the scars of that fateful night would never fully heal - the Square slowly began to regain its sense of safety and security.

Life carried on but the memory of Geordie who was killed in the doorway would forever serve as a reminder of the senseless act of violence.

Deb was forced to move on and was rehoused in a new home with her children. We did our best to support her and her children through the horrific trauma she had experienced.

Nana Nell turned her home into a shrine to her son Geordie and grandson John. Their photographs were displayed in grandly embellished frames and huge bunches of fresh flowers displayed throughout the house which were renewed every week.

Nana Nell maintained her gangster status and started to control Deb's life and that of her children. Nana Nell always favoured Geordie and Deb because she was able to manipulate and control them, but her love for them caused a lot of jealously within the family.

Drew and I moved into our house and we started looking to the future. Others chose to wallow in the attention generated by the killing of Geordie and relished in their newly found status

This terrible event made me reflect on my own life. Looking back my love for my Dad had never diminished but our relationship had become fractured. I wanted to rebuild and reignite my relationship with him. A relationship that Mam had done her level best to wilfully destroy for many years.

As we renewed our relationship I would meet Dad and Uncle Claude at their club and join them for a chat and a beer or occasionally we would meet at Dad's flat. We never talked about the past and what Mam had done or how she had lied. We just talked about the here and now and the future.

Uncle Claude had been unwell for a long time and had moved to a bungalow because of ill health and also because Grandma and Grandads house was to be demolished. Although Uncle Claude had taken some of Grandma and Grandads possessions with him to his bungalow he left lots behind. One of those things was his Wedding album. I was devastated because I loved that album.

One of my deepest, happiest childhood memories was looking at Uncle Claude's and Auntie Jeanie's wedding albums. Uncle Claude was married in the 1960's in St Bartholomew's Church. I remember his album was quite luxurious and the outer cover was made of crocodile skin. There were rice paper sheets separating the beautifully coloured pictures.

I remember sitting on the edge of the bed for what seemed like hours, turning the beautiful pages and admiring the pictures. It was like a fairy tale. Auntie Jeanie wore the most gorgeous short wedding dress at her wedding. I always said that if I got married I would wear a short wedding dress and when I married, I did!

Uncle Claude gave me some of Grandma and Grandad's possessions and I still absolutely cherish them and always will. They serve as a reminder of the nicer times and the nice things that have happened in my life and help to dilute some of the awfulness.

Crime Scene

Heartbreak Hospital

Chapter 22

Health and Heartbreak

It was around 2002/3 that Dad started to experience some difficulties with his mobility. At the beginning he started to drag one of his feet as he was walking and then, as things progressed, he started to trip and fall over. Dad knew that something was seriously wrong and sought medical advice. After a series of tests over many months his consultant was able to give him a diagnosis. I was supporting Dad and with him in the hospital when he was given his diagnosis.

The news was devastating! Dad had Motor Neurone Disease (MND). The consultant calmly and carefully explained that MND was not like a cancer where, with treatment, it could improve or even be cured. He told us there was no cure for Motor Neurone Disease. The condition was terminal.

Dad asked the consultant how long he had left to live. The consultant looked at Dad and told him as compassionately as he could that there was no definitive answer to his question but he gave an indication that the likely time was eighteen months from diagnosis. We were stunned. Absolutely stunned. We couldn't speak, we didn't know what to say or what to do. For just a moment it seemed like time stood still.

We stood up and left the room. We slowly walked along the hospital corridors, holding onto each other and not speaking a word until we stepped outside. Tears were rolling down Dads face and mine too. He rolled a cigarette and took long - deep puffs. I told and assured Dad I would never leave him and I would always be there for him.

To this day I don't know how I managed to get Dad back to his house. All I remember was a sense of injustice that he was ill, terminally ill. He was never going to get better. I felt a huge gaping hole in my heart at the thought of losing Dad. My emotions were numb.

We went back to Dad's house together. As soon as we walked through the door he broke down and sobbed, he didn't want to die, he wanted to live. Whilst Dad was still sobbing, and for the first time, he said to me "Do you mean to tell me that Joe was coming to my house when I was working away"? I couldn't lie so I said "yes". He said "why didn't you tell me"? I said "Dad, we were children, you and Mam were the adults". We both just sat and cried and cried. My dad was facing death, he had just been given the worst and most awful news and it is at this point he is able to ask me about, what I can only believe was his most awful fear and that was what Sylvie had done to all of us.

The hospital had organised a special MND nurse called Jill to assess Dad's needs and to make regular visits to him. She was lovely and Dad got on well with her. It was reassuring and comforting to know that professionals were looking after him as well as me.

I talked to Dad a lot and he told me that he had sought the support of a psychiatrist to help him cope with Mam's narcissistic, manipulative and aggressive behaviours. I hadn't realised how much Dad as well as me and my brothers had been impacted by her. Dad felt, because trauma can be a factor in MND, that it was because of the way Mam had behaved that he was now suffering with MND. On reflection, I, too, blame my kidney problems and anxiety on Mam's toxic behaviour.

Drew and I worked together to support Dad in whatever way we could. We organised adaptations to his home to help him cope with daily activities and would take him out when it was possible. I would take him to his club on a night time and then go back and pick him up, taking him up two flights of stairs using a piece of equipment called a stair walker.

Each week Dad was deteriorating, his strength was diminishing and he was becoming weaker and weaker. He so wanted to live. His mind was completely active but his body was shutting down.

The first major impact on Dad was that he lost the use of his legs and this was quickly followed by losing the use of his arms. Drew and I wanted to do whatever we could to help Dad keep his independence and to make his life as comfortable as we could. We managed to get him an electric chair and then, as he continued to deteriorate, we moved him to a ground floor flat within supported accommodation and right next door to where he was living.

The move to supported accommodation gave me and Drew some peace of mind that 24-hour support was available if Dad needed it and there was specialised equipment on-site to help move him. Dad was comfortable in his new accommodation and was keen to take part in any research to find a cure for MND. He became involved in a clinical trial. Dad didn't want to die. I didn't want him to die and between us we agreed that we would do anything we could to make life as good as it could be. Drew was always supportive and would help in any way he could.

Sylvie, although not involved in Dad's care, was always buzzing around in the background, asking about Dad's health status and whether he had a Will. I could hardly believe it but money was always her priority.

Dad talked to me about what he wanted to happen when he had passed. He had made a Will and had named me as Executor. His money was to be shared equally between me, Robert and Alfie but he had put in a special clause which stated that the contents of the Will could not be activated until the death of Sylvie and on the production of her death certificate. I was completely shocked and said I thought it was awful as it would mean that we would have lost both parents. I understood why he had included that clause but I was still shocked. Dad reconsidered and had the clause removed.

Dad's condition was now rapidly deteriorating. I was visiting and supporting him daily. Robert, now a wealthy business man, followed Mam's instructions and visited Dad occasionally. Mam's mission was to ensure that Robert got the inheritance she thought he should have. Alfie on the other hand was in a such chaotic state he rarely visited Dad.

When I next visited Dad, he told me that he had changed his Will again. I was still Executor but he was leaving everything to me, for me to decide what I wanted to do with it. He said Robert didn't need any money and Alfie wasn't in a fit state or responsible enough to have any money.

I asked Dad not to change his Will in this way as Robert and Alfie would hate him and I knew Sylvie probably already had plans for the money. Sylvie honestly thought that Dad should leave her money. She even went to visit him and tried to influence him to change his Will to favour her. Her visit must have been so difficult for him. He still loved her but he was vulnerable, immobile and dying. Sylvie knew this and yet she still went to see him and tried to coerce and manipulate the whole dreadful situation.

Money was never important to me. My Dad was so much more important. Sylvie however craved money. She would go to great lengths to acquire it because it helped to open doors, build friendships and broaden her horizons.

The last few weeks and days of Dad's life were really difficult, very emotional and traumatic. Watching someone you love develop paralysis and lose their ability to speak whilst their mind remains alert is heart-breaking.

Mam became very resentful of the relationship I had with Dad and became furious when she realised that was not being left anything in the Will. Her resentment and how she would respond weighed heavily on my shoulders.

Dad was now struggling to breath and his respiratory system was shutting down. The medics decided he now needed specialist care in hospital as he had contracted pneumonia. It was horrible watching Dad struggle to breath yet desperately wanting to cling onto life. The hospital told us that they would not resuscitate him if his condition deteriorated.

Dad was determined to live as long as he could and kept clinging on to life. One-night Robert picked me up to go to the hospital. When we got to Dad's bedside we could see that he was upset which made me upset. After just a short while Robert said he had to leave saying something like he was busy so, because I was a passenger in his car, I had to leave too. I wasn't happy and didn't feel comfortable about leaving Dad so upset.

On the drive home with Robert I said that we shouldn't have left Dad when he was so upset. Robert stopped the car almost immediately, right on the carriageway and shouted at me to get out. I was shocked at his anger and quickly got out, not understanding why he should have asked me to get out. He drove off at speed. I could not believe it. I was already upset at leaving Dad in a state and now I had been abandoned on a motorway in the middle of no-where. I phoned Drew and gave him some clues as to the location and he came, found me and we went home.

I tried to work out why Robert responded in the way that he had. Maybe he felt guilty at not seeing more of Dad. Maybe he was struggling to come to terms with the difficult situation we were all in and with the prospect of losing Dad. Maybe he had now realised the impact that Mam had had on all of us, but, honestly, I don't really know. What I do know is that a few short days later Dad had a slow and agonising death. He died with Alfie and me by his side.

I was distraught, devastated. I went home and was consoled by Drew. That night, in my disturbed sleep, I could see an image of Dad floating above and in front of me saying "April, there was nothing more you could have done". I awoke in a sitting position gently blowing Dad away like a cloud.

I carried out Dad's final wishes and gave him a Catholic burial. A Sottish bagpiper piped Amazing Grace as he was gently laid to rest. I organised his Wake to take place in his favourite club. I remember suddenly feeling overwhelmed by the enormity of his absence.

Sylvie was at the Wake and hanging around like a vulture ready to strike its prey.

I grieved for my lovely Dad. A Dad who wanted to be a Dad and who taught us right from wrong, who wanted the best for us even though Sylvie tried to stop him and put her needs first.

Part of my grief, which remains with me to this day, is the sense of injustice for my Dad. He was put through torture by Sylvie and she prevented me from spending vital time with him, time I will never get back. It was such a torrid time and it unleashed Sylvie's deep hatred of me. She hated that I had cared for my Dad and that we had been able to have a close relationship. A relationship that was not influenced, controlled or manipulated by her.

Dad endured and suffered the cruel torture of Motor Neurone Disease. A disease that stripped away his ability to move and communicate but never diminished his incredible humanity.

He died when he so wanted to live. Our remaining time together was special but cut short and ultimately controlled by a terminal illness. His spirit and legacy will always and forever guide me, reminding me to be kind, to forgive and to never let the past define the future.

Dad once told me that his one and only regret was "ever having us born into my Mam's family".

Sylvie held our family captive with her lies, manipulation and deceit. We have all been scarred by a woman called Sylvie.

Dad at the park

Acknowledgements

I would like to thank Jay who is a very special person. You have restored my faith in humanity. You have given me the confidence, encouragement and support to put my story into words and for never letting me forget my hopes and dreams. Without your commitment, time and expertise this book would never have been possible.

I owe an enormous debt of gratitude to those I call "The Good People" who have been part of my world for decades and have changed the course of my life for the better.

Jossie and Chrissie, deserve special words of appreciation, your strength, love and support showed me an alternative way of life.

Drew, when you became part of my life you changed my world forever. I thank and love you.

M. Jade, you enrich my life always and forever lovely girl.

Picture Credits

- Authors own pictures
- Newcastle Evening Chronicle
- Shutterstock

Milton Keynes UK
Ingram Content Group UK Ltd.
UKHW041842090224
437425UK00006B/111

9 781835 380956